Chinese Home-Style Cooking

Edited by Bai Ziran
Written by Wang Jinhuai and Xue Yuan

FOREIGN LANGUAGES PRESS   BEIJING

First Edition 1990
Eighth Printing 2007

Chinese Editor : Bai Ziran
Chinese Contributors : Wang Jinhuai and Xue Yuan
English Translator and Editor : Tan Manni
Photographers : Wei Dezhong, Zeng Xianyang, Sun Suxian, Sun Chun,
              Hang Lukue and Tong Jiannan
Layout : Li Wei and Yan Xinqiang
Illustrator : Li Wei

ISBN 978-7-119-00407-5

© Foreign Languages Press Beijing, 1990
Published by Foreign Languages Press
24 Baiwanzhuang Road, Beijing 100037, China
Distributed by China International Book Trading Corporation
35 Chegongzhuang Xilu, Beijing 100044, China
P.O. Box 399, Beijing, China

Printed in the People's Republic of China

CONTENTS

AUTHOR'S FOREWORD

There was a time when it was the custom in North China families that every new bride should make her debut in the kitchen on the third day after her wedding. As the future cook of the household, she was expected to begin showing off her culinary repertoire by first making flour noodles and some accompanying dishes. If she displayed mastery in kneading, rolling and cutting the dough, she would win the admiration of the other young women of her neighbourhood.

Today, the roles in Chinese families have changed. Women are no longer the only cooks; both husbands and wives are not only breadwinners but also share the household chores. Husbands today must learn cooking skills so they, as well as their wives, can serve varied and tasty meals to their families. Also, family gatherings and parties can become occasions when couples can display their cooking skills as a team—though often it is still the wife who shows the greatest mastery.

For example, I remember meeting Liu Zhaoxia, a very accomplished homemaker and cook, when I was invited by her husband, a photographer, to a family party at their home in the province of Guizhou. Liu Zhaoxia, whose photograph is on the inside front cover of this book, was a young woman of great intelligence. She also had a great hunger for learning. Although she was born and raised in Guizhou and had never seen Shanghai, she had learned Shanghai dialect and spoke it fluently. She also took so ardent a liking to Shaoxing Opera, a form popular in Zhejiang Province and Shanghai, that she became an actress with the local Shaoxing opera troupe in Guizhou. Still later, when she unfortunately lost her voice, she soon learned sign language and taught art in a school for deaf-mutes.

But what most surprised me that first afternoon was her cooking. She bustled around the kitchen and eventually produced a series of about a dozen different dishes which made a colourful spread on the table. After I sampled her food, I was even more impressed. I was astonished by the way she had managed to give each dish a different character. Some featured purely local ingredients while others were specialties selected from the cuisines of North and South China—but all approached perfection in colour, aroma, taste and appearance.

And Liu Zhaoxia was by no means an exception; there are many Chinese husbands and wives who can cook as expertly as she could.

The origins of China's cuisines date back thousands of years. The land is so vast that eight distinctive cooking styles developed —in the provinces of Sichuan, Shandong, Guangdong, Jiangsu, Hunan, Fujian and

"Pandas Playing in Bamboo Grove," prepared with hair seaweed (fa cai), crab meat and cucumber peels.

Anhui, and the capital city of Beijing—to take advantage of the many different local foods available.

However, all these regional styles originated in everyday cooking long before they diverged along their unique paths. Family-style cooking is basic to Chinese cuisine; though the regional styles are distinguished by local ingredients and different techniques, all eight have one thing in common: they all use the freshest foods available and rely on simple, uncomplicated ways of preparing them.

In recent years, the cuisines of China have received high praise from foreign tourists. Visiting Chinese from overseas have come looking for the foods and flavours of their hometowns and for special dishes characteristic of other regions of their motherland. Many want recipes they can try out for themselves once they return home, but some well-known dishes are too complicated, and family-style recipes have not been available.

It is for this reason that we are publishing this book. We hope it will be of help to every reader, but especially to homemakers abroad who want to cook Chinese food.

The focus of this book is on family-style Chinese cooking. It includes recipes chosen from all the different cooking styles of North and South China. The recipes use everyday ingredients and simple techniques easily within the grasp of most homemakers. The illustrations are of actual dishes created by Chinese housewives. However, we have also included recipes for some of China's most celebrated dishes. Although their preparation is more time-consuming and involves many more steps, they are not as complicated as they may appear at first glance, and you may wish to try them when you want to regale your family or guests with a special feast.

Note: MSG (monosodium glutamate) is a flavour enhancer; its use in the following recipes is optional.

"Goldfish in Water," prepared with thousand year-old eggs, eggs and red cherries.

Chinese Cooking Techniques

Xue Yuan

Chinese cooking has a long history. It was the Chinese who invented the technique of making and using soy sauce, vinegar, wine, jams, and spices during the Yin-Zhou period, some 3,000 years ago. They were also using a wide variety of cooking techniques. By the Spring and Autumn (770-476 B.C.) and Warring States (475-221 B.C.) periods, the Chinese people began to study cooking techniques and produced books on food preparation. For example, *Master Lü's Spring and Autumn Annals*, written in the third century B.C., discussed temperature control and the balancing of seasonings, describing them as two key aspects of cooking.

Chinese cuisine aims for perfection and balance among four elements in each dish: colour, aroma or fragrance, flavour, and presentation. Colours should be pleasing, showing that the ingredients are fresh and tender. Aromas should be appetizing and flavours enticing. Finally, the dish should be beautifully arranged and presented. Good Chinese cooking is also distinguished by its meticulous cutting, careful blending of seasonings, and attention to temperature control.

This chapter offers a brief description of some of the basic techniques, skills, and ingredients of Chinese cooking. I hope it will be helpful to readers when they try the recipes that follow.

Selecting Ingredients

Chinese cooking uses a wide range of ingredients, including meat, meat products, fish, seafood, poultry, eggs, vegetables, bean products, wild plants, game, and many seasonings. Most come in both fresh and dried forms, but the most important features to look for are freshness and quality.

Meats should be judged by their place of origin, season of production, and any other characteristic—for example, old or young, male or female—that may be specified in a recipe. Appearance, colour, weight, water content, and smell are also important.

Different dishes call for different cuts of meat because cuts have different textures once they have been cooked. Cuts of the same meat may be tough or tender, coarse or fine. For example, the Chinese distinguish eighteen different cuts of pork. These include filet, streaky pork, shoulder butt, ham butt, hock, and shank.

The filet is considered the best cut and is generally stir-fried or quick-fried (see the section below on "cooking techniques" for descriptions of these and other procedures) to take advantage of its tenderness. Streaky pork is best when marinated with spiced rice flour (see recipe 24) and then steamed, or red-cooked (braised in soy sauce). The shank and hock are best suited to lengthy simmering, with or without soy sauce, while the ham and ham butt are often used as substitutes for filet. The ribs and feet are best prepared by lengthy, low-temperature methods like braising, baking or simmering, while spareribs are suitable for sautéing, quick-frying, slippery-frying, and deep-frying. The methods used for pork are also applicable to similar cuts of beef and lamb or mutton.

With reference to poultry, the tenderest and most versatile part of a chicken or duck is the breast. Chickens or ducks less than a year old are usually quick-fried or deep-fried, while older birds need long, slow cooking like simmering or braising to tenderize them.

Fish is as nutritious as poultry. Crab,

prawns and shrimps are rich in phosphorus, calcium and vitamin A. You can tell a fresh fish by its tight, undamaged scales, red gills, and clear protruding eyes. Fresh prawns and shrimps should be greenish-white, with firm bodies that curve slightly. They should not be flat or limp, and their heads and tails should be intact. Fresh crabs should be alive and active. They should spit foams and have green upper shells and white under-shells.

Preparation

In Chinese cooking, preparation includes trimming and washing vegetables, slaughtering and dressing live chickens and ducks, gutting live fish, and reconstituting dried ingredients.

When preparing vegetables, cooks first trim and discard any wilted or tough outer leaves. Then they wash them. Vegetables should not be cut before they are washed, because vitamins and minerals would be washed away. Nutrients are also lost if vegetables and other foods are cut ahead of time and exposed to the air. The most nutritious dishes are prepared and cooked immediately.

Chinese cooks prefer to buy live poultry and fish and to kill them themselves whenever possible because they believe that freshly-killed chickens, ducks and fish have a subtler flavour. If you slaughter your own poultry, you should drain off the blood thoroughly and soak the bird in very hot water before plucking it. When preparing a duck, you will find it easier to pluck the eiderdown if you force-feed it with wine, vinegar, or cold water before killing it. To draw a bird, make an incision about 3 inches (7 cm) long along the lower part of the breast, on the back, or under one of the wings. When drawing out the entrails, be careful not to puncture the gallbladder; its bitter taste would ruin the edible meat. Then wash the bird thoroughly before continuing to prepare the recipe.

Preparing a fresh, whole fish involves scaling, chopping off the fins, taking off the gills, gutting and washing. To gut the fish, make a cut along the belly or spine and take out the black membrane in the belly cavity. If the recipe calls for a whole boned fish, you should first gut it by cutting along the spine. Then cut parallel to the spine almost up to the top and separate the flesh from the top and bottom of the center bone. Lift out the center bone and small side bones and cut the spine away at the head and tail. Finally, wash the cavity and the outside and arrange the fish as closely as possible in its original shape.

The easiest way to shell shrimps and prawns is to hold the head in one hand and the tail in the other hand and squeeze the meat out of the shell at the neck end. Wash the vein away under cold running water or pick it out with the tip of a knife. Wash the shrimp, drain, dry well, and set aside. Sometimes shrimp and prawn heads are also used in dishes.

Drying makes meats, seafoods and vegetables tough and fibrous. To reconstitute dried foods, first soak them in cold water until they soften. Then soak them

in warm water until they expand and regain their original texture and pliability.

When preparing dried vegetables such as wood ear (an edible fungus) or golden needles (also known as dried tigerlily buds), you need not use cold water first. Wash the vegetables well to remove any dirt or sand, and then soak them in hot water until soft. Dried black Chinese mushrooms are prepared the same way, but require less soaking time.

Cutting

Chinese recipes call for ingredients to be cut into different shapes because different ways of cutting affect the texture and appearance of a finished dish.

Chinese cooks use three main cutting techniques (see illustrations): straight-cutting (also known as perpendicular-cutting), horizontal-cutting (slicing), and slashing (scoring). Both straight-cutting and slicing are used to create chunks, slivers, slices, strips, cubes, and even pulps and pastes. Slashing means making shallow parallel cuts on the surface of an ingredient, usually a meat or fish. This exposes a larger area to the seasonings and to the heat source. If an ingredient is scored in a crisscross or diamond pattern, it will shrink to form a raised flower-shaped pattern when cooked.

Balance Among Ingredients

Chinese cooks attach great importance to the balance among the ingredients in a dish. This important step should result in a harmonious blending of textures, colours, aromas, flavours, shapes and nutritional qualities. To do this well, you must understand the required cooking methods of the dishes and the characteristics of different ingredients and how they fit together.

Balancing amounts The major ingredient should be the most plentiful one in a dish. If you are making stir-fried meat shreds, for example, the total quantity of other ingredients should not exceed the amount of meat. If there are two or more main ingredients, you should use about the same amount of each.

Balancing flavours All the ingredients in a dish should enhance the flavour of the main ingredient. This is why asparagus or bamboo shoots are often cooked with chicken, duck, and fish: the blandness of these vegetables enhances the light, delicate character of the meat.

Similarly, the blandness of shark's fins and sea cucumbers (*beche-de-mer*, sea slug) can be offset by cooking them with Chinese ham, chicken, or pork, or in a highly-flavoured stock. You can also cut the heavy, greasy character of a main ingredient by adding lighter secondary ingredients. This is why many Chinese recipes call for pork to be cooked with fresh vegetables.

You must also take seasonal factors and personal preferences into account. Summer is the season for light, juicy foods, while heavier dishes, or ones with thick gravies, are better suited to cold weather. When you plan a menu, you should balance sweet, salty, sour, and hot dishes to suit your taste and that of your family and guests.

There is also a Chinese sequence for serving dishes: salty dishes are served before sweet ones, while heavy- and light-flavoured ones are served alternately.

Balancing textures Texture refers to the crunchiness, crispness, softness, or tenderness of a food. In Chinese cooking, ingredients with similar textures are usually cooked together. However, crisp and soft foods are sometimes combined in a single dish. This requires careful attention to cooking temperatures to retain the differences in textures.

Balancing shapes Chinese cooks usually cut all the ingredients in a dish into similar shapes. For example, chunks of meat and chunks of vegetables are usually cut to about the same size. This makes it easier to cook all the ingredients evenly and also gives the final dish a pleasing appearance.

Balancing colours Chinese cooks tend either to select ingredients of the same colour, or to use many contrasting ingredients to add colour to a dish.

Blending Seasonings

A well-prepared dish should have a distinctive flavour. But it is not enough just to select the right blend of foods and the correct cooking temperature—a good cook also needs to master the art of blending the right seasonings with the right combinations of ingredients. Without the correct seasoning, even delicious ingredients can taste bland and uninteresting. Seasonings are also important in Chinese cooking because they create the special flavours that characterize different regional styles.

The condiments used in Chinese cooking come in two ways, singly or blended. They lend single flavours (salty, sour, sweet, etc.) or blended flavours (sweet and sour, sweet and salty, hot and spicy, etc.) to foods. Some examples of these flavours and the condiments used to create them are:

Salty flavour is basic to most dishes, with other flavours usually added. Salt and soy sauce are the main seasonings used to impart a salty taste.

Sweet flavours counteract fishy odours, cut the greasiness of rich dishes, and enhance delicate flavours. The main seasonings use to give a sweet flavour to foods are confectioner's sugar, brown sugar, rock sugar, granulated sugar, honey, and saccharin.

Sour flavours help the digestion and increase the absorption of inorganic salts. They also lighten heavy or rich dishes. Red and white rice vinegar are the main seasonings used to add sourness to a dish.

Hot flavours are appetizing because of their sharpness. Hot seasonings include fresh and dried red chili (chilli) peppers, pepper, ginger, scallion, and garlic.

Bitter flavours have a special aftertaste that can be palatable and refreshing. Ingredients such as bitter melon, Chinese yam, tangerine peel, and Chinese wolfberry give a bitter flavour to dishes.

Spicy flavours help mask off-odours or fishy smells, cut greasiness, and whet the appetite. In Chinese cooking, the main spicy condiments are cassia bark, which resembles cinnamon, star anise, fennel, clove, Sichuan red peppercorns, sesame, sesame oil, sesame paste, wine, red wine mash and flavouring essence.

The first five spices are often ground and mixed together into a combination called "five-spice powder."

Delicate flavours are natural food essences, generally the principal amino acid of the ingredient. Shrimp eggs, crab meat, oyster sauce, fish sauce, and meat stock impart delicate flavours.

Sweet and sour flavour comes from sweet and sour sauce, a mixture of sugar and vinegar, jam, and ketchup (catsup).

Sweet and salty flavour comes from a combination of shrimp eggs, soy sauce, and shrimp paste.

Peppery and salty flavour comes from mixtures like the combination of roasted

"Braised Fresh Mushrooms and Hyacinth Beans."

ground Sichuan peppercorns and salt known as "spiced pepper-salt."

Spiced pepper-salt is sometimes referred to as "prickly ash." One basic recipe for making it is:

4 tbsp salt
1 tbsp whole Sichuan peppercorns

Heat a dry wok over moderate heat and pour in the peppercorns.

Cook, stirring constantly, about 1 minute, or until they release their fragrance. Grind to a fine powder in a mortar or blender, strain out any large husks, and set aside. Reheat the wok and pour in the salt. Cook, stirring constantly, about 5 minutes, or until it just begins to turn golden brown. Pour into a bowl and let cool slightly before mixing with the ground peppercorns. Store in a tightly-closed jar. Makes about 1/4 cup and will keep indefinitely.

Sharp and salty flavour is obtained from chili (chilli) peppers or Sichuan peppercorns and salt.

Hot and spicy flavour comes from seasonings like curry and mustard.

Hot and salty flavour is found in condiments like chili (chilli) sauce and Worcestershire sauce.

Seasonings can be added to foods before, during, and after cooking. Because the success of Chinese dishes depends so much on how they are seasoned, the following guidelines may be helpful.

Fish, shrimp, beef, lamb, and mutton sometimes have off-odours. Adding wine, vinegar, scallions, ginger, or sugar before or during cooking helps counteract unpleasant odours.

Do not over-season dishes that feature delicate foods like fish, shrimp, chicken, duck, or mushrooms, or you will kill their flavour.

Bean threads (also known as "cellophane noodles"), shark's fin, and sea cucumbers are so bland that they should always be cooked with a highly-flavoured sauce or stock.

The amount of seasoning used should be correct. When a dish has several flavours, the principal and complementary flavours must be balanced to enhance the principal flavours.

The predominant flavours of Chinese dishes change with the seasons. Fresh, crunchy foods and sweet-and-sour cold dishes are best for hot weather, while winter is the time for heavier, fattier dishes, or those that call for long, slow cooking techniques like stewing or braising. Hot pot, in which a variety of fresh ingredients and meat is cooked in a boiling broth in a special cooking pot, is also a special cold-weather dish.

Cooking Techniques

Chinese cooking has developed many methods that take advantage of the wide range of foods and ingredients available throughout the nation. Different regions use different methods, and often the same foods will be prepared quite differently.

The basic techniques used in Chinese cooking are precooking techniques such as parboiling and partial frying, and cooking techniques such as frying, sauté-ing, braising, stewing, boiling, simmer-ing, steaming, "flavour-potting," and smoking. This section also describes cook-ing temperatures, cooking with oil, mari-nades, sugar and other coatings, sauces, gravies, stocks and flavouring sauces.

Precooking Methods

Some meats need to be partially pre-cooked just long enough to get rid of off-odours but not so long their flavour or texture changes. Some vegetables also need precooking to get rid of astringency or bitterness or to heighten their fresh colour. Parboiling and partial frying are the two most common methods of pre-cooking foods before they are combined with other ingredients for the remaining steps in a recipe.

Parboiling: There are four methods of parboiling. Each uses different timings and temperatures and yields different results.

Parboiling vegetables like taro root, Chinese yams and fresh bamboo shoots by cooking them in boiling water before they are cooked with other ingredients, helps to remove their astringent taste and makes peeling easier. These vegetables should be parboiled in their skins, if possible, and peeled and cut as required afterwards to avoid loss of nutrients.

Slow-boiling is used for foods like pork tripe that take a longer time to cook than the other ingredients in a recipe. These foods should be simmered in boiling water until tender and then combined with the

rest of food and seasonings called for in the recipe.

Hot-plunging or *blanching* is used for some tender, fresh vegetables to set their colour and texture. Celery, spinach, green beans and other vegetables are plunged into a large pot of boiling water and removed as soon as the water returns to a boil. They are then drained and run immediately un-der cold water to stop the cooking process.

Quick-boiling is often used to rid meat of bits of bone and the off-odour that comes from the blood. The meat is placed in cold water and removed and drained as soon as it comes to a boil. However, the method used for pork kidney, fish, and chicken is closer to blanching: the meat is dropped into boiling water and removed as soon as it is cooked.

Chinese cooking also uses two methods of *partial frying* foods as an intermediate step in many recipes.

Sliding through the oil means placing an ingredient in warm oil which has been heated to 158° to 212° F (70° to 100°c) just long enough to seal in the juices.

Going through the oil means deep-frying ingredients, usually meats, in hot oil, (275°-300°F, or 110° to 170°c) until partial-ly or thoroughly cooked, depending on what the recipe specifies.

Cooking Temperatures

Heat is what causes all the changes that take place in foods when they are cooked. Because different temperatures and cooking times lead to different results, temperature control is a key element in Chinese cuisine.

Chinese recipes call for three kinds of heat: high heat, used in stir-frying, quick-frying, and deep-frying; medium heat, used in sautéing, slippery-frying, and deep-frying coated foods; and low heat, used in steaming, simmering, braising, and stewing.

Chinese recipes also often specify three levels of flame (or heat, on the electric ranges which are common in the West) to regulate the levels of heat of water.

High flame or heat is used to produce a fast boil, in which the water or liquid is kept bubbling rapidly. The fast boil is used to reduce and thicken broths or stocks and in hot-plunging and quick-boiling.

Medium flame or heat keep liquids at a moderate boil and is used in some types of braising.

Low flame or heat is used to keep liquids at a slow boil or simmer in stewing, simmering, and flavour-potting.

Cooking with Oil

Many of the recipes in this book call for deep-frying foods in large amounts, from two to eight cups (500 ml to two litres), of vegetable oil. When foods are deep-fried at the proper temperature, they absorb very little oil, but, it can be difficult to judge whether oil is at the right temperature.

Although many Chinese recipes call for oil to be heated "to the smoking point" when deep-frying, it should be pointed out that the cooking oils used in China are often less highly refined than those used in the West. The presence or absence of impurities changes the appearance of oil as it heats.

We therefore suggest using thermometers to gauge how hot oil is.

Warm oil is about 160° to 210°F (70° to 100°C). In this temperature range, no bubbles will appear around a small piece of vegetable leaf like a piece of scallion green or spinach, or a slice of ginger, that has been tossed into the oil.

Moderately hot oil is about 230° to 340°F (110° to 170°C). In this temperature range, small bubbles will sizzle around a piece of ginger, or scallion tossed into the oil.

Very hot oil is about 350° to 420°F (180° to 220°C). At 350°F, a one-inch cube of day-old bread will turn brown in one minute when dropped into the oil.

Boiling oil is above 420°F (220°C). A heavy haze appears and the oil bubbles vigorously.

Most Chinese recipes call for oil to be heated to the hot or very hot stage. Lower temperatures are used in methods like sliding through the oil, while extremely hot oil is used to crisp and brown coated foods that have already been fried at a lower temperature.

Coatings

Chinese recipes often call for meats and other ingredients to be first marinated and

"The Red Tangerine Is Ripe," prepared with shrimp meat and mushrooms.

then dipped into a batter—a paste which may contain cornstarch or flour, egg white, salt, sugar, and monosodium glutamate. When the food is later deep-fried, the coating seals in juices, keeps the food from falling apart, and reduces the loss of nutrients. These coatings also cook into light, crisp crusts that contrast with the tenderness of the food inside.

Cooking pastes and coating are also used for foods that will be stir-fried, quick-fried or slippery-fried because they impart a soft, slippery quality to the dish.

The most common batter is made of *cornstarch and water*. It is usually made of two parts cornstarch to one part water and is used in deep-frying and slippery-frying. It cooks into a crisp, yellowish-brown crust when deep-fried.

A batter of egg white and cornstarch is used in stir-frying and slippery-frying. The batter remains white after cooking, but the food inside is tender.

An egg yolk and cornstarch batter may also be used in deep-frying and slippery-frying. It results in a golden-brown coating.

The flour and egg yolk coating is actually a two-step process. The food is first dipped in flour and then into beaten egg yolk.

Another two-step process is *egg and bread-crumb coating*. The food is first dipped in beaten egg yolks and then rolled in bread crumbs. When deep-fried, the coating turns crisp and golden-brown.

Cooking Methods

Frying:

Chinese cooking uses many methods of frying, including several types of deep-frying, "slippery-frying," "quick-frying," and several types of stir-frying.

In *deep-frying* (*zha*), ingredients are fried in four to six cups of vegetable or peanut oil over a high heat.

In *dry deep-frying* (*gan zha*), foods are given a thick coating of cornstarch (cornflour) before being fried. They come out very crisp outside and tender inside.

In *clear deep-frying* (*qing zha*), the foods are not coated with cornstarch before being cooked.

In *flaky deep-frying* (*su zha*), foods are parboiled or steamed until they are almost cooked through. Then they are dipped in a thick batter of cornstarch and water and cooked in boiling oil until the coating turns crisp and flaky.

In *soft deep-frying* (*ruan zha*), the ingredients are not precooked, but are given a light coating of cornstarch before being fried. They come out tender but not crisp.

Chinese cooking also uses two techniques for deep-frying ingredients in wrappers.

In *paper-wrapped deep-frying* (*zhibao zha*), the food is wrapped in sheets made of

13

glutinous rice flour.

In *crisp deep-frying* (*cui zha*), the wrappers are made of dry bean-curd sheets.

Both methods involve first deep-frying the packets of food in moderately warm oil over a high heat and crisping them by frying them briefly when the oil comes to a boil.

Slippery-frying (*liu*) involves two processes. The ingredients are deep-fried and then covered with a cornstarch-based sauce prepared in a separate pot during the frying or immediately afterward. When the sauce is poured over the food, it results in a texture as slippery as satin. Foods prepared this way are fragrant, crisp, and tender.

In *deep-frying before stir-frying* (*peng*), foods are deep-fried in very hot oil until cooked. Then the excess oil is poured out and a sauce which unlike slippery-frying does not contain cornstarch is added. The dish is stir-fried for a few moments to blend the ingredients before being served. Dishes prepared this way are crisp outside and tender inside , with each morsel covered in a velvety sauce.

In *quick-frying* (*bao*), foods are deep-fried in very hot oil over high heat and then the oil is poured out and seasonings are added to the food, which is left in the wok.

Chinese cooking distinguishes four types of *stir-frying* (*chao*). In all four types, ingredients are cut into small cubes, strips, shreds, or slices, and cooked over high heat in a few tablespoons of very hot oil in a wok. The technique of stir-frying involves using a flat scoop to toss and turn the ingredients so they cook evenly in the oil. Sometimes the wok is also shaken. Stir-frying usually takes only a few minutes. The food must be removed as soon as it is cooked to guarantee its fresh flavour and crunchy-tender texture.

In *raw stir-frying* (*sheng chao* or *bian*), raw ingredients are quickly stir-fried, resulting in a fresh, tender dish with little sauce.

In *stir-frying pre-cooked food* (*shu chao*), the ingredients are parboiled or precooked before being stir-fried.

In *soft stir-frying* (*ruan chao*), the food to be stir-fried is coated with a batter before being cooked.

There is also *stir-frying without coating* (*gan chao*).

Sautéing

Chinese cooking uses three methods of sautéing, which is also called "shallow-cooking." Sautéing uses much less oil than deep-frying and is done at lower temperatures than stir-frying. Ingredients are usually cut into slices or flat pieces. Seasonings are added after the food is browned.

In *sautéing on both sides* (*jian*), foods are browned slowly on both sides in oil but do not have a coating.

Sautéing on one side (*tie*) means browning batter-coated foods on one side only.

In *sautéing followed by cooking in sauce* (*ta*), foods are coated in a batter and sautéed on both sides. Then a sauce is added and the dish is simmered until the sauce thickens. The food will be soft inside, but with some crispness outside, and the thickened sauce will be slippery.

Braising, Stewing, Boiling and Simmering

Chinese cooking has many methods of cooking foods in liquids.

Stewing one kind of meat (ao) means slow-cooking chunks, slices, cubes, or shreds of meat after first stir-frying them briefly until the surfaces have lost their raw look but before the insides are cooked. Seasonings and broth are added and the liquid is brought to a boil. Then the heat is turned down and the meat simmers slowly until done. The sauce is not thickened.

In *precooking before stewing (hui)*, several ingredients are parboiled or precooked before being placed in one pot for slow simmering. Unlike *ao*, the final step involves thickening the sauce.

Stewing over low heat (men) resembles braising. The meat is stir-fried briefly to brown. Then seasonings and a sauce are added and the dish simmers over low heat until the sauce is almost all reduced.

Stewing over medium, then high, heat (shao) means braising foods over medium heat until tender, then turning the heat to high to reduce the sauce.

Both of the above methods can be applied to "red-cooking," or braising in soy sauce. The soy sauce imparts the reddish look that gives this technique its name.

Stewing meats with bones (ju) is similar to the above methods, but the meat or poultry is first marinated in rice wine and soy sauce. Then it is deep-fried before being simmered in sauce and water. The meat is not boned.

Stewing and adding thickening (pa) is similar to stewing meats with bones, but the sauce is thickened with cornstarch instead of being reduced and thickened by simmering.

In *quick-boiling in broth (cuan)*, thinly-sliced ingredients are cooked quickly in a boiling clear broth, or in water.

In *dip-boiling (shuan)*, as with the "hot pot" dishes referred to earlier, diners pick up morsels of meat, seafood and vegetables and cook them by dipping them into boiling water or stock in a fire-pot.

Boiling (zhu) simply refers to cooking ingredients in a large amount of water over high heat. The sauce is reduced and the food comes out tender. No cornstarch is used. The gravy or sauce is rich but light and fresh.

In *simmering (one of several forms of dun)*, foods are put into cold water and brought to boil. Then seasonings are added and the heat is reduced for long, slow cooking.

Simmering over high heat (wei) also starts with cold water, as in *dun*, but the food is cooked at high heat over a long period. This method tenderizes tougher meats and poultry and yields a thick, heavy sauce.

In *simmering over charcoal (wo)*, the food is cooked over very low heat from a charcoal burner for three or four hours. This gives it a delicate flavour and a soft, tender texture.

Steaming

Chinese cooking uses two methods of steaming, or cooking foods over, rather than in, liquids.

In *basic steaming* (*zheng*), the ingredients are placed in a heat-proof container with a seasoned sauce. Then the container is placed in a steamer partially filled with water and set over high heat. The food cooks quickly in the vapor and is removed when barely done. The result is fresh and tender.

Another form of steaming involves *placing one tightly-closed pot inside a larger pot* (*steaming dun*). In this method, the ingredients, a seasoned sauce, and a large amount of stock go into one pot, which must have a tight-fitting lid. The pot is half-immersed in boiling water in another larger pot and steams for two or three hours. The result is very soft.

Flavour-Potting

This method refers to stewing foods in a highly-flavoured sauce (see the section on "Stocks and Flavouring Sauces" below) that permeates the dish.

Basic flavour-potting (*lu*) means stewing the food in a mixture of soy sauce, rice wine, sugar, salt, red fermented rice mash, and five-spice powder, scallions, ginger, chicken stock and water. The food cooks over low heat for several hours and comes out tender and full of flavour.

Marinating and flavour-potting (*jiang*) adds the step of marinating the food in salt, soy sauce, and soybean paste (also known as ground bean sauce) before it is stewed in the flavour-potting sauce.

Smoking

Chinese cooking treats smoking and roasting as similar methods.

In *smoking* (*xun*), foods are parcooked and then cured in smoke from burning wood or peanut shells.

In *roasting* (*kao*), raw ingredients are marinated in seasonings before being roasted in an oven or barbecued over direct heat from a coal or charcoal burner.

Marinades

Marinades are an essential part of many Chinese recipes and marinating may take place before or after ingredients are cooked.

In *ban*, raw foods or those that have been cooked and cooled are cut into small pieces and mixed with soy sauce, vinegar, and sesame oil. Other seasonings, such as garlic, ginger, sesame paste, sugar, or ground peppercorns, may also be added to heighten the flavour.

In *qiang*, the main ingredient in the marinade is peppercorn oil, mixed with other seasonings and poured over foods that have first been parboiled or partial fried.

The *yan* method of marinating uses salt-water brine, water, or liquor. In salt-marinating, the food is soaked in brine, which draws out the moisture from the food so it can better absorb the seasonings in the marinade that follows. Wine-marinating is similar to salt-marinating, but uses fermented rice liquor instead of seasonings in the marinade.

Finally, the Chinese speciality called "drunk-marinating" means soaking live food, especially seafood such as shrimps, in a clear liquor and then marinating them in salt. Then the food is often eaten while still alive (see recipe #95, "Drunken Fresh Shrimps").

Sugar and Syrup Coatings

Chinese cooking has three methods of coating foods with sugar or syrups.

In *spinning a thread of syrup (basi)*, the ingredients are deep-fried or boiled before being dipped into sugar that has been melted in either oil or water and cooked until it thickens and spins a thread.

In *preserving in syrup (mizhi)*, foods are partially cooked and then boiled in a sugar and honey sauce until the syrup thickens.

In *coating with frost (guashuang)*, foods are cooked by deep-frying while sugar is melted with water or oil in another pot to make a white syrup. When the food is mixed with the syrup, it looks as if it is covered with a layer of frost.

Sauces and Gravies

Thickening the liquids in the pan into a sauce or gravy is often the last step in a recipe, and can be crucial to the success of a dish.

Sauces are made either by stirring a mixture of cornstarch that has been dissolved in an equal amount of water into the liquid and cooking it until it thickens, or by making a sauce or gravy in another pan and pouring it over the dish just before it is served.

Sauces help blend the flavours of all the ingredients, impart an added aroma, and give the dish a shiny, glistening finish.

Chinese recipes usually rely on two kinds of gravies. The first is a mixture of cornstarch, soy sauce or salt, sugar, vinegar, MSG, and a little water. It is usually used for stir-fried and slippery-fried dishes and is added to the pan at the last stage of cooking.

The other way to make gravy is to add seasonings gradually while the dish cooks and to thicken it at the last minute with cornstarch and water. This lets the flavours of the seasonings permeate the food and is generally used with long, low-heat cooking methods.

Stocks and Flavouring Sauces

First or *prime stock* is made by simmering chicken, Chinese ham with bone, salt, and water for several hours.

Secondary stock is made by simmering the meats from the prime stock a second time with salt and water.

Seasoned sauce is prime stock with sugar, salt, sesame oil, and pepper added.

Clear stock is made by boiling chicken and duck carcasses with salt and water.

High stock is clear stock with pork hocks and ham shanks added. Two recipes for flavour-potting sauces are:
Superior Flavour-Potting Sauce

> 4 tsp vegetable oil
> 4 tsp sliced ginger
> 4 cups (1 litre) soy sauce
> 2 cups (500 ml) rice wine
> 3 tbsp scallions, chopped

14 oz (400 g) rock sugar

21 cups (5,000 ml) water

a cheesecloth bag containing 1 oz (25 g) each of star anise, cassia bark (Chinese cinnamon, or substitute regular stick cinnamon), licorice root, ground dried ginger, caoguo, cloves, and dried tangerine peel.

Bring water to a boil in a large saucepan, add spices, simmer for 15 minutes. Add soy sauce, rice wine, sugar and oil stew for one hour.

Flavour-Potting Sauce

2 cups (500 ml) soy sauce

4 cups (1 litre) water

7 tsp rice wine

3 tbsp sliced ginger

1 tsp (5 g) each of star anise, cassia bark or cinnamon, and whole Sichuan peppercorns,

Stew the soy sauce, rice wine, ginger and seasonings with the water.

Chopsticks

Chopsticks, used to lift food to the mouth, are basic to Chinese table settings. The historical record shows that the Chinese have been using chopsticks since the eighteenth century B.C. In 1974, a pair of chopsticks dating back two thousand years was unearthed in an ancient tomb in South China.

Early chopsticks were much longer than modern ones, which measure about 10 inches (25 cm) long, because the bronze tripods, quadripods, and pottery vessels used for foods then were deeper and had wider rims than food containers today.

Today, chopsticks are usually made of wood or bamboo. Sometimes they are made of ivory or silver. They can be plain, or lacquered and painted with floral or other designs. It is said that emperors and empresses in feudal times used chopsticks made exclusively for them. A pair of these chopsticks, painted with the royal symbols of the coiling dragon and flying phoenix, took a skilled craftsman a month to make.

The most sought-after chopsticks nowadays are plain bamboo ones, painted with views of the scenic West Lake, from Tianzhu, near Hangzhou, lacquered ones from Fujian, and ebony ones made of the black, hard wood found in Guangxi Province. The latter are known for their durability as well as their beauty—they will not warp, even after long use.

Chinese children learn to use chopsticks

at a very early age and can manipulate them quite easily by the time they are five or six.

To learn to use chopsticks, perch them between the thumb, first, middle, and ring fingers so they lie parallel to each other. The lower chopstick rests on the inside tip of the ring finger, which keeps it stationary, while the thumb, first, and middle fingers manoeuvre the upper chopstick in a pincer movement to pick up the food. Dexterity comes with lengthy practice—if you can pick up a pea and carry it to your mouth, you can call yourself an expert with chopsticks.

Individual pairs of chopsticks are placed neatly at the right side of the plate or bowl, at a right angle to the edge of the table. They should not stick out over the table edge because they might fall to the floor. Chinese table settings also often include a second pair of chopsticks, called common chopsticks, which are used by the diners to transfer food from the serving dishes to their own plates or bowls. These chopsticks are placed in front of the diners' plates and parallel to the table edge. After a meal, chopsticks should be left neatly on the table. It is considered bad manners to toss one's chopsticks carelessly on the table after dining.

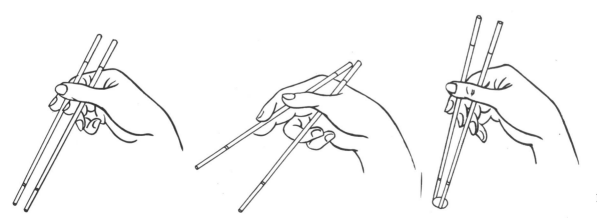

Bamboo strainer

Perforated spoon

Bamboo steamer or assembled metal steamer

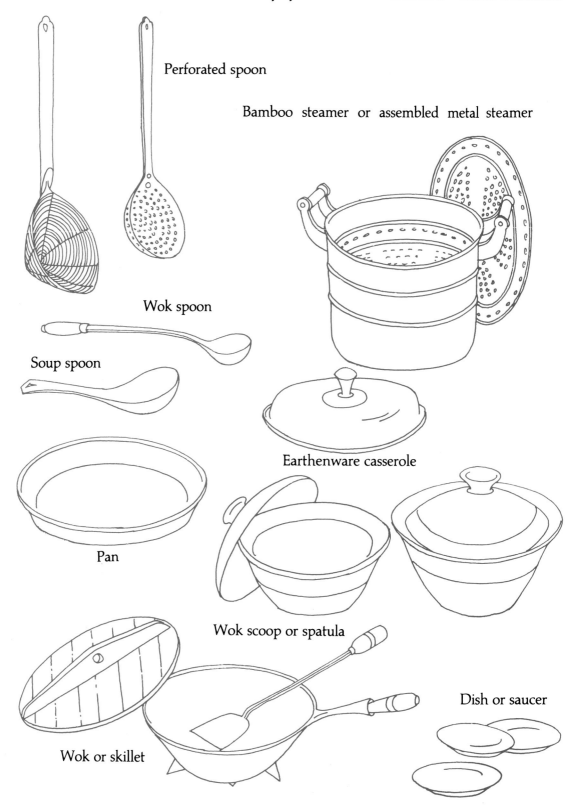

Wok spoon

Soup spoon

Earthenware casserole

Pan

Wok scoop or spatula

Dish or saucer

Wok or skillet

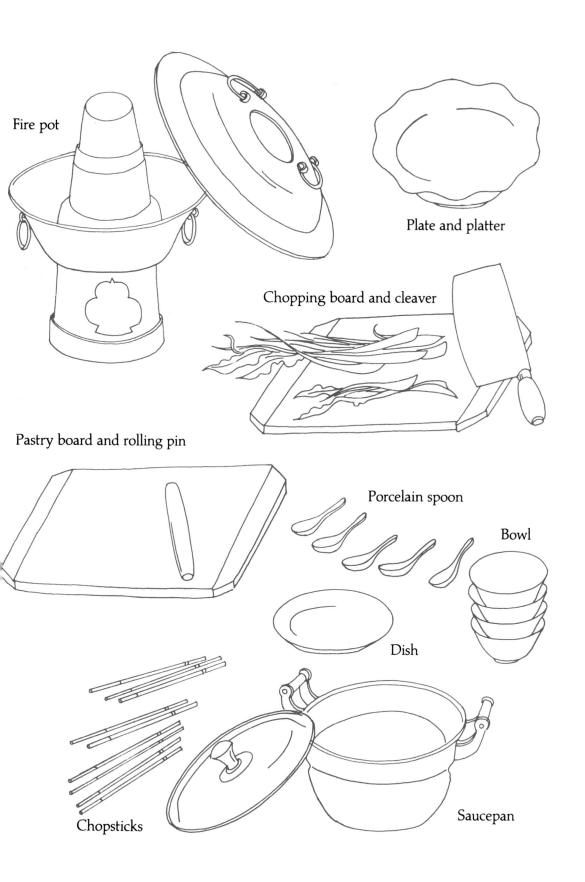

Fire pot

Plate and platter

Chopping board and cleaver

Pastry board and rolling pin

Porcelain spoon

Bowl

Dish

Chopsticks

Saucepan

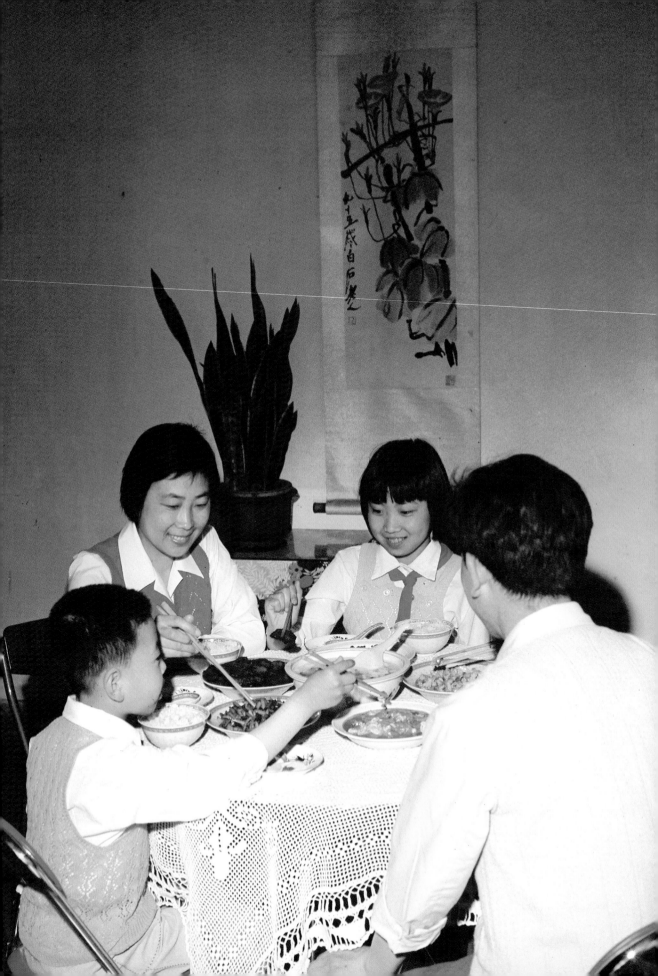

Recipes

PORK DISHES

1. Twice-Cooked Pork, Sichuan Style

1 lb (450g) fresh boneless pork or fresh, uncured ham
3 oz (80g) scallions or garlic shoots
1 tbsp vegetable oil

2 tbsp soybean paste
1 tbsp sweet bean sauce
1/4 cup meat stock

1. Wash the pork, drop it into boiling water to cover, and parboil for 8 minutes. Remove, drain, and cut into slices about 2 inches long by 1 1/2 inches wide and 1/4 inch thick (7 cm by 4 cm by 16 mm). Set aside.

2. Cut the scallions on the slant into 1 inch (3 cm) pieces. Set aside.

3. Heat the oil in a wok to very hot 356°F (180°C), or until smoke rises on the surface. Add the pork slices, soybean paste, sweet bean sauce, scallions or garlic shoots, and stock. Stir-fry for 5 minutes, or until the scallions are tender and the soybean paste loses its raw taste. Remove and serve.

2. Muxi Pork, Beijing-North China Style

1 oz (25 g) wood ears, reconstituted
1 oz (25 g) golden needles
3 1/2 oz (100 g) lean boneless pork
1/2 tsp fresh ginger, minced
1 tsp cornstarch (cornflour)
2 tsp soy sauce
3 eggs

5 oz (150 ml) vegetable oil
1 tsp rice wine
1 tsp salt, or to taste
1 oz spinach, cut into 3 inch (7 cm) pieces
1/2 tsp sesame oil
1/4 tsp MSG

1. Wash the wood ears and drain. Soak the golden needles in warm water for 5 minutes. Drain and cut crosswise into halves. Set aside.
2. Wash the pork and cut it into slivers. Mix with the soy sauce, ginger, and cornstarch, and set aside.
3. Beat the eggs and mix with 3/4 tsp salt. Scramble the eggs in 5 tbsp of the oil and set aside.
4. Heat 4 tbsp of the oil in a wok over high heat to very hot, add the pork slivers and stir-fry for about 30 seconds, or until the meat is partially cooked. Stir in the rice wine. Remove the pork and set aside.
5. Heat the remaining 1 tbsp oil in the wok. Add the golden needles and wood ears and stir-fry for 30 seconds. Add the 1/4 tsp salt, MSG, and spinach pieces. Stir-fry until the spinach leaves darken slightly. Add the pork slivers and scrambled egg. Stir-fry another few seconds to blend the ingredients. Sprinkle with the sesame oil, remove, and serve.

3. Stir-Fried Pork Cubes with Green Peppers, Beijing Style

4 1/2 oz (125 g) boneless pork shoulder
1 oz (20 g) peanuts, skinned and deep-fried
1 tsp salt, or to taste
6 egg whites
4 tsp (20 g) cornstarch (cornflour)
3 tbsp meat stock or water
1 tsp rice wine
1 tsp soy sauce

1/4 tsp scallions, chopped
1/4 tsp ginger powder
1/4 tsp garlic, sliced
1 1/2 tsp sugar
3 tbsp vegetable oil
2 oz (50 g) green pepper, seeded and cut into
    1/2 inch (1 cm) cubes
1/4 tsp hot chili

1. Wash the pork, cut into 1/2-inch (1.5 cm) small cubes, and mix with 1/2 tsp salt. Beat the egg whites and mix with 3 tsp of the cornstarch. Add the pork cubes and mix to coat well. Set aside.
2. Mix the stock with the remaining 1 tsp of cornstarch, 1/2 tsp salt (or to taste), rice wine, soy sauce, scallions, ginger, garlic, and sugar. Set aside.
3. Heat the oil in a wok to moderately hot (230°F or 110°C). Add the pork cubes and stir-fry for about 30 seconds, cooking them just long enough to seal in the juices. Remove, drain, and set aside. Pour out the oil from the wok and reheat. Add the green peppers and stir-fry for 30 seconds. Then add the pork cubes. Stir the sauce to blend it, then add to the wok. Add the peanuts and hot chili oil. Bring to a boil and cook, stirring, until thickened. Remove and serve.

4. Stir-Fried Hot Diced Pork, Beijing Style

5 oz (150 g) boneless pork loin or shoulder, with lean and fat
1 tsp crushed yellow bean sauce
2 tsp cornstarch dissolved in 2 tsp water
3 1/2 oz (100 g) cucumber
1 oz (25 g) fresh chili (chilli) peppers, seeded
2 cups (500 ml) vegetable oil for deep-frying

(about 4 tbsp/50 ml will be used)
1 tsp (5 g) scallions, minced
1/2 tsp (3 g) ginger, minced
1/4 tsp salt, or to taste
1 tbsp stock
2 tsp rice wine

1. Wash the pork and cut it into 1/2 inch (1 cm) cubes. Mix with the crushed yellow bean sauce and the 2/3 of the cornstarch and set aside.
2. Cut the cucumber, chili peppers and scallions into 1/2 inch (1 cm) pieces. Set aside.
3. Heat the oil in a wok to very hot about 390°F (200°C), or until a piece of scallion or ginger dropped into the oil turns brown quickly and a haze appears above the oil. Deep-fry the pork cubes until barely cooked, stirring the pieces to keep them from sticking together. Remove, drain, and set aside.
4. Pour the oil out of the wok, leaving only enough to cover the bottom, about 5 tsp. Reheat the oil until very hot, add the scallions, ginger, salt, cucumbers, chili peppers, and stock. Stir-fry a few seconds, then add the pork cubes and rice wine. Stir-fry several times, then stir 1/3 of the cornstarch-water mixture to blend and add to the wok. Cook, stirring, until the sauce thickens. Remove and serve.

5. Steamed Pork with Fermented Bean Curd, Suzhou Style

1/2 lb (200 g) pork, lean and fat, cut in a
  square with skin attached
1/2 tsp (3 g) red fermented rice
1 oz (25 g) red fermented bean curd
1 oz (25 g) rock sugar, crushed

3/4 tsp salt
1 tsp scallion sections
1/2 tsp fresh ginger, chopped
2 tsp rice wine

1. Place the pork in boiling water to cover. Drain and wash in hot water. Cut into 1-inch (4 cm) squares.

2. Soak the red fermented rice in a little warm water, crush it, and mix with the fermented bean curd, rock sugar and 1/2 tsp salt into a paste. Coat the pork slices with the paste.

3. Stack the pork slices, skin side down, in a large bowl and pour the rest of the paste over them. Add the scallion, ginger, and rice wine. Cover the bowl tightly with a dish. Place the bowl in a steamer and steam over boiling water for 3 hours over a high fire, adding water when necessary, until the meat becomes very tender. Remove the bowl from the steamer. Discard the scallions and ginger. Cover the bowl with a serving dish and invert both so the pork slide into the dish with the skin side up. Serve.

6. Steamed Pork with Fermented Bean Curd, Guangdong Style

1 1/4 lb (600 g) pork, lean and fat with skin
1 1/2 tsp soy sauce
4 cups (1 litre) vegetable oil for deep-frying; will use about 1/2 cup (100 ml)
14 oz (400 g) potatoes, peeled and cut in 1/8 inch (4 mm) slices
3 cakes fermented bean curd
1 1/2 tbsp scallions, chopped

1 tbsp fresh ginger, chopped
1 1/2 tbsp garlic, chopped
3 cups (750 ml) chicken broth
2 tsp rice wine
1 tsp salt, or to taste
1 tbsp sugar
1 tbsp cornstarch (cornflour) dissolved in 1 tbsp water

1. Wash the pork and boil in water until thoroughly cooked. While the pork cooks, deep-fry the potato slices until cooked, drain, and set aside. Drain the pork and coat the skin with soy sauce.
2. Deep-fry the pork in hot oil, 350°F (180°C) until the skin browns. Drain and soak in cool water until the skin becomes soft. Then cut into 1/8 inch (4 mm) slices, leaving some skin on each slice.
3. Crush the fermented bean curd into a paste and set aside.
4. Heat 2 tbsp of oil in a wok to very hot. Add the scallion, ginger, and garlic, and stir-fry. Add the bean curd and stir-fry briefly, then add the pork slices and stir-fry 30 seconds. Add the chicken broth, rice wine, salt, soy sauce, and sugar, and stir to blend. Bring to a boil, lower the heat, and simmer slowly until the pork is tender.
5. Remove the pork slices and stack in a large, heat-proof bowl with the skin side down. Pour sauce from wok over meat and set the bowl in a steamer. Steam over high heat for 5 minutes.
6. Pour sauce back into wok, place pork in a serving dish, skin side up. Arrange potatoes around meat.
7. Heat the sauce, stir the cornflour-water mixture to blend it, and add to the sauce. Cook, stirring, until thickened. Pour over the pork and serve.

7. Shredded Pork, Sichuan Style

5 oz (150 g) boneless pork filet
3/4 oz (20 g) pickled chili (chilli) pepper
1/4 tsp salt, or to taste
1 tbsp soy sauce
2 tsp rice wine
4 tsp cornstarch (cornflour)
4 tbsp (50 ml) vegetable oil

2 tsp rice vinegar
4 1/2 tsp sugar
2 tsp scallions, chopped
1 tsp fresh ginger, chopped
1 tsp garlic, chopped
1/2 tsp pepper
1/4 tsp MSG

1. Cut the pork and chili pepper into slivers. Set the peppers aside. Mix the pork with the salt and 1 tsp each of the soy sauce and rice wine. Mix with 1 1/2 tsp of the cornstarch and a few drops of oil and stir to coat.
2. Mix 2 tsp of the soy sauce, vinegar, sugar, the remaining 2 1/2 tsp of cornstarch, the remaining 1 tsp of rice wine, the scallion, ginger, garlic, pepper, and MSG into a sauce. Set aside.
3. Heat the oil in a wok to very hot. Add the pork slivers and peppers and stir-fry until the pork is cooked through. Add the sauce and stir-fry about 30 seconds, or until blended and thickened. Remove and serve.

8. Peppery-Hot Pork Slices, Sichuan Style

9 oz (250 g) lean boneless pork
1 egg white, beaten slightly and mixed with
   a little flour into a paste
1/4 tsp salt, or to taste
1 tbsp hot soybean paste
1 tbsp soy sauce
1/4 tsp sugar
1/2 tsp fresh ginger, chopped
1 1/2 tsp cornstarch (cornflour) dissolved in
   1 1/2 tsp water

1/4 cup meat stock
2 cups (500 ml) vegetable oil for deep-frying;
   uses about 5 oz (150 ml)
3 1/2 oz (100 g) Chinese cabbage hearts (bok
   choy), sliced.
1/2 tsp Sichuan peppercorns, crushed
1 tbsp hot chili (chilli) oil
2 tsp sesame seeds, roasted and ground
1/4 tsp MSG

1. Cut the pork into slices about 2 inches by 1 inch by 1/8 inch (5 cm by 26 mm by 4 mm). Mix with the egg white paste and 1/8 tsp of the salt. Set aside.
2. Mix the soy sauce, sugar, ginger, MSG, cornstarch, and stock into a sauce and set aside.
3. Heat 2 tbsp of the oil in a wok to moderately hot, add the cabbage and 1/8 tsp salt, stir-fry until cooked. Remove, drain, and set aside.
4. Add the rest of the oil to the wok and heat it to about 230°F (110°C). Add the pork slices, stirring to keep them from sticking together. Cook until done, remove, and drain well.
5. Pour the oil out of the wok and reheat it. Add the peppercorns and soybean paste and stir-fry until the peppercorns turn purplish-red. Add the pork, sauce, chili oil, and ground sesame seed, and stir-fry until the sauce thickens. Pour the meat and sauce over the cabbage hearts and serve.

9. Dry-Fried Pork Filet, Beijing-Hebei Style

7 oz (200 g) boneless pork filet
2 tsp soy sauce
1 tsp rice wine
3 tbsp cornstarch, dissolved in 3 tbsp water

2 cups (500 ml) vegetable oil for deep-frying
3 tbsp spiced pepper-salt (see p. 10)
1/4 tsp MSG

1. Cut the pork into diamond-shaped slices, 1 1/2 inches (4 cm) in each side. Mix with the MSG, soy sauce and cornstarch and stir to coat well.
2. Heat the oil in a wok to very hot about 400°F (200°C), or when a piece of scallion or ginger tossed into the oil quickly turns brown and a haze appears above the oil. Deep-fry the pork until the coating becomes crisp. Remove the pork, drain and let stand for 2 minutes while reheating the oil to 400°F. Place the pork back in the oil for a few seconds, remove immediately and serve with the spiced pepper-salt as a dip.

10. Yuanbao Pork, Beijing-Hebei Style

9 oz (250 g) lean and fat pork loin with skin
5 tsp soy sauce
2 cups (500 ml) vegetable oil; uses about 1/4
cup (50 ml)
1 clove of star anise, crushed

1 tsp fresh ginger, chopped
1 tsp scallions, chopped
1 tbsp rice wine
1/4 tsp salt, or to taste
4 eggs, hard-boiled

1. Boil the pork in water to cover until barely cooked. Remove, drain, and coat with 1 tsp soy sauce.
2. Heat the oil in a wok over a medium fire to very hot, 430°F (220°C), add the pork and deep-fry until small bubbles appear on the skin. Remove and let cool. Then cut into slices, 1/8-inch (4 mm) thick, leaving some skin on each slice. Stack the slices in a heat proof bowl, skin side down.
3. Sprinkle the star anise and ginger over the pork. Mix together with the rice wine, salt, and 3 tsp of soy sauce, and pour over the pork. Place the bowl in a steamer and steam over boiling water until thoroughly cooked, about one hour.
4. While the pork steams, shell the eggs and soak them in 1 tsp soy sauce for 10 minutes. Reheat the oil to moderately hot and deep-fry the eggs until golden brown. Drain, let cool slightly, and cut into halves.
5. Cover the bowl containing the pork with a serving dish turned upside down. Invert the bowl so the pork slides onto the dish with skin side up. Arrange the eggs around the pork and serve.
Note: This dish gets its name from the eggs, which resemble *yuan pao*, the gold ingots used as money in ancient times.

11. Steamed Pork Balls, Hangzhou Style

4 1/2 oz (125 g) pork, 1/3 lean, 2/3 fat or
    commercially-ground pork
1 egg white, beaten slightly
1/2 tsp rice wine
1/2 tsp salt, or to taste

1 tsp cornstarch (cornflour)
7 oz (200 ml) stock
2 oz vegetable leaves
1/4 tsp MSG

1. Mince the pork if it is not already ground. Add the egg white, rice wine, MSG, and salt, and stir to mix. Add the cornstarch and mix well. Shape lightly into four equal-sized balls.
2. Pour the stock into a wok and bring to a boil. Add the meat balls and cover them with the leaves. Bring to a boil over high heat, then turn the heat down, and simmer for 1 hour, or until the meat is tender and the gravy has thickened. Remove and serve.

12. Pearly Pork Balls, Beijing-Hebei Style

9 oz (250 g) pork, 1/3 lean, 2/3 fat, or com-
  mercially-ground pork
1 tbsp soy sauce
1/2 tsp salt, or to taste
1 tsp rice wine
2 eggs, beaten

1 1/2 tsp sugar
2 tbsp cornstarch, dissolved in 2 tbsp water
1/2 tsp scallions, chopped
1/2 tsp fresh ginger, minced
3 oz glutinous rice
1/4 tsp MSG

1. Mince the pork if not already ground. Mix with the 1/4 tsp salt, soy sauce, MSG, rice wine, eggs, sugar, cornstarch, scallions, and ginger. Set aside.
2. Wash the rice in several changes of water until the water runs clear. Then pour boiling water over it and drain.
3. Lightly shape the meat mixture into balls about 1 inch (25mm) in diameter and roll them in the rice, covering them completely.
4. Mix the 1/4 tsp salt (or to taste) with the rice that remains and spread it in the bottom of a large heat-proof bowl. Place the meat balls on the rice and set the bowl in a steamer. Steam for 25 minutes over high heat, then turn the heat to low and steam 10 minutes more, or until the pork is cooked. Remove and serve.

13. Pork Balls in Clear Broth, Sichuan Style

9 oz (250 g) lean and fat pork
1 egg, beaten
1/2 tsp scallions, chopped
1/2 tsp ginger, chopped
2 tbsp cornstarch (cornflour) dissolved in 2 tbsp water
4 cups (1 litre) meat broth
2 tsp salt, or to taste
1 oz (25 g) wood ears, reconstituted in hot water

1 oz (25 g) golden needles, soaked in hot water
2 oz (50 g) Chinese cabbage hearts, coarsely chopped
2 oz (50 g) cellophane noodles (flour or bean threads), soaked in warm water
1 tsp sesame oil
1/4 tsp ground Sichuan peppercorn
1/4 tsp MSG

1. Mince the pork, if not already ground, and mix well with the scallions, ginger, egg, corn starch, 3 1/2 fl oz (100 ml) of the broth, and 1/2 tsp of the salt.
2. Heat the remaining broth to a boil, then turn the heat to low. While the broth is heating, make small meatballs, about 3/4-inch (2 cm) in diameter.
3. Add the meatballs to the broth one by one, and simmer until done.
4. Skim the foam from the broth and add the wood ears, golden needles, cabbage hearts and cellophane noodles. Bring to a boil and add the pepper and MSG, sprinkle the sesame oil on the broth, remove, and serve.

14. Four Happiness Pork Balls, Beijing Style

3 1/2 oz (100 g) Chinese yam, peeled (or substitute potatoes)
14 oz (400 g) lean and fat pork
2 tsp rice wine
1 tsp soy sauce
2 tsp salt
1 tsp fresh ginger, chopped

1 egg, beaten
3 tbsp (50 g) cornstarch (cornflour)
9 oz (250 ml) vegetable oil for deep-frying
1 tsp scallions, chopped
1 large fennel (substitute 1 clove of star anise)
2 cups (500 ml) meat stock
1/4 tsp MSG

1. Boil, peel and mash the yam or potato. Mince the pork and mix with the yam mash, MSG, rice wine, 1 tsp of the soy sauce, salt, and 1 tsp of the ginger. Stir in one direction until the pork and yam paste stiffens, then shape it lightly into four flattened balls. Mix the egg, cornstarch, and 1 tsp soy sauce into a paste and coat the balls.

2. Heat the oil in a wok over medium heat to moderately hot, 212°F (100°C). Deep-fry the meatballs until they are reddish-brown, drain, and place in a heat-proof bowl.

3. Add the scallion, the remaining 3/4 tsp ginger, the fennel, and the stock, and place the bowl in a steamer. Steam the meatballs until done. Discard the scallions, ginger, and fennel. Remove and serve.

15. Stir-Fried Pork Slices with Scallions, Shandong Style

7 oz (200 g) lean boneless pork
7 oz (200 g) scallions
4 tbsp vegetable oil

1 tbsp soy sauce
5 wood ears, reconstituted in hot water
1/4 tsp MSG

1. Cut the pork into slices about 1 1/4 inch by 5/8 inch by 1/8 inch (3 cm by 16 mm by 8 mm). Cut the scallions diagonally into 1 1/4-inch (3 cm) sections.
2. Heat the oil in a wok to very hot, 350°F (180°C). Add the pork slices and stir-fry for 30 seconds.
3. Add the soy sauce, wood ears, MSG, and scallions. Stir-fry for 2 more minutes, remove, and serve.

16. Stir-Fried Diced Pork with Peanuts, Guangdong Style

10 1/2 oz (300 g) lean boneless pork
1 tsp cornstarch (cornflour) dissolved in 1 tsp water
2 1/2 tbsp seasoned sauce (see p. 17)
1/2 tsp soy sauce
1/2 tsp sesame oil
a dash of ground Sichuan peppercorn

3 cups (750 ml) vegetable oil for deep-frying; uses about 1/4 cup (60 ml)
1/2 tsp scallions, chopped
1/4 tsp garlic, chopped
1 tsp rice wine
7 oz (200 g) skinned peanuts, deep-fried until golden

1. Cut the pork into small cubes and mix with 1/2 tsp of the cornstarch.
2. Mix the seasoned sauce, soy sauce, 1/4 tsp sesame oil, the rest of the cornstarch and the pepper into a sauce. Set aside.
3. Heat the oil in a wok over high heat to very hot. Deep-fry the pork cubes until cooked, remove and drain.
4. Pour the oil out of the wok, leaving only enough to cover the bottom. Reheat to very hot, and add the scallion, garlic, rice wine and peanuts. Stir-fry until blended, and add the pork cubes. Pour in the sauce and stir until thickened. Sprinkle 1/4 tsp sesame oil over it, remove and serve.

17. Stir-Fried Pork Slivers with Ginger, Shanghai Style

4 oz (125 g) lean boneless pork
1 oz (25 g) pickled ginger (or substitute fresh ginger)
1/2 oz (15 g) green pepper
5 oz (150 g) mung bean sprouts
7 tsp vegetable oil
1/4 tsp rice wine

2 tsp soy sauce
1 1/2 tsp sugar
1/2 tsp salt, or to taste
2 tsp cornstarch (cornflour) dissolved in 1 tbsp water
1/4 tsp MSG

1. Cut the pork into thin slivers about 2 1/2 inches (65 mm) long.
2. Rinse the preserved ginger, cut it and the green pepper into shreds about 2 1/2-inches (65 mm) long. Remove roots of mung bean sprouts. Wash and drain thoroughly.
3. Heat 4 tsp of the oil in a wok to very hot. Add the pork slivers and stir-fry until cooked. Add the rice wine, soy sauce, and sugar, and stir several times to blend. Pour into a bowl and set aside.
4. Add the remaining 1/3 tsp oil to the wok, and reheat to very hot. Add the ginger, green pepper, and mung bean sprouts and stir-fry several times. Return the pork mixture to the wok and stir in the salt and MSG. Stir the cornstarch mixture to blend and pour into the wok. Cook, stirring, until thickened. Remove and serve.

18. Sweet-and-Sour Pork, Guangzhou Style

1 lb (500 g) lean and fat boneless pork
1 tsp salt, or to taste
2 eggs, beaten
3 tbsp plus 1 tsp (50 g) dry cornstarch (corn-flour)
1 medium green pepper
7 oz (200 g) bamboo shoots
4 cups (1 litre) vegetable oil for deep-frying
4 tsp garlic, sliced
2 tbsp scallions, chopped

For the sauce:
4 1/2 tbsp sugar
3 tbsp vinegar
2 tsp soy sauce
2 tbsp tomato ketchup
1 cup (120 ml) water
1/4 tsp salt, or to taste
2 tsp cornstarch (cornflour) dissolved in 2 tsp water

1. Wash the pork and cut into diamond-shaped slices about 1 inch (25 mm) long. Mix with the salt and let stand for 15 minutes, then mix well with the eggs and dry cornstarch.
2. Halve vertically, seed and wash the green pepper. Cut the green pepper and the bamboo shoots into diamond shapes, the same size as the pork. Set aside.
3. Heat the oil in a wok over medium heat to very hot, about 375°F (190°C). Deep-fry the pork slices until they turn golden brown and float to the surface. Drop the bamboo shoots into the oil and remove immediately, along with the pork. Drain well and set aside.
4. Make the sweet-and-sour sauce in another pot.
5. Pour the oil out of the wok, leaving only enough to cover the bottom, about 2 tbsp. Heat to very hot, or until the oil surface ripples. Add the garlic and stir-fry. Then add the scallions and green pepper and stir-fry for 1 minute. Add the sweet-and-sour sauce and bring to a boil. Stir the dissolved cornstarch to blend and add to the wok. Cook, stirring, until thickened. Add the pork. Stir to coat thoroughly. Remove and serve.

19. Braised Fresh Ham with Rock Sugar, Sichuan Style

4 lb (1,000 g) fresh, uncured ham, boneless
3 1/2 oz pork bones
10 cups (2 litres plus 500 ml) pork stock
4 tbsp (60 ml) rice wine
1 tbsp fresh ginger, sliced

1 tbsp scallions, chopped
3 1/2 oz (100 g) rock sugar
1 oz (25 g) brown sugar
2 tsp salt, or to taste

1. Wash the ham and the bones and place in a large wok with bones under the ham. Add the stock and bring to a boil over high heat. Skim the foam from the surface and add the rice wine, ginger slices, scallions, sugars, and salt. Simmer, tightly covered, over low heat until the ham is tender. Discard the bones and place the ham in a serving dish.
2. Bring the sauce back to a boil and reduce until thickened. Pour over the ham and serve.

20. Deep-Fried Fresh Ham, Shandong Style

1 lb (500 g) fresh boneless uncured ham
5 tbsp soy sauce
3 oz (100 g) scallions, chopped
a thumb-sized ginger, crushed
3 1/2 tbsp rice wine
7 tbsp (100 g) cornstarch (cornflour)
one egg, beaten

1/2 tsp salt, or to taste
8 cups (2 litres) vegetable oil for deep-frying;
    uses about 3 1/2 oz (100 ml)
3 oz whole scallions
1/4 tsp ground Sichuan peppercorn
14 tbsp (100 g) sweet fermented flour paste
    or sweet bean sauce

1. Boil the ham in water to cover until the colour changes from pink to white. Remove, drain and rinse in cold water. Cut into 13 slices and stack in a large, heat-proof bowl in the ham's original shape.
2. Blend together 3 tbsp of the soy sauce, the chopped scallions, ginger, and 2 1/2 tbsp of the rice wine and pour over the ham. Place in a steamer and steam for 1 hour. Remove the ham, drain, and set aside.
3. Mix together the cornstarch, egg, salt, and the remaining 1 tbsp of rice wine and 2 tbsp of soy sauce into a batter. Coat the ham thoroughly on all sides with the batter.
4. Heat the oil in a wok to very hot, about 375°F (190°C), or until a piece of scallion green or ginger sizzles noisily and quickly turns brown when tossed into the oil. Turn the heat down and carefully add the ham without letting it fall apart. Deep-fry until the exterior is hard, turn the heat to high, then deep-fry until the exterior browns. Turn heat to low. When the oil no longer sizzles and bubbles, remove the ham and drain well. Then cut the slices apart and place them on a dish in a "U" shape. Sprinkle with the ground peppercorns.
5. Cut the scallions into 2 inch sections and arrange them along one side of the meat. Spread the sweet bean sauce along the other side as a dip.
Note: The ham will have a crisp exterior but will be tender inside. Though fat, the flavourful meat will not taste greasy.

21. White-Boiled Pork with Mashed Garlic, Chongqing-Sichuan Style

9 oz (250 g) boneless pork or uncured ham
2 cups (500 ml) pork stock
2 oz (50 g) garlic, peeled and pounded to a paste

1/4 tsp sesame oil
3 tbsp plus 1 tsp soy sauce
1/4 tsp chili (chilli) oil

1. Wash the ham and boil in water to cover until done.
2. Drain and cut into three strips. Soak them in the stock for 5 minutes to absorb the flavour, then cut the strips into thin slices.
3. Mix the garlic with the sesame oil, adding enough water to make a paste. Blend the paste, with the soy sauce and the chili oil. Pour it over the pork, blend well, and serve.

22. Cauliflower with Chinese Ham, Beijing Style

1 whole cauliflower, about 3/4 lb (400 g)
1 2/3 cups (400 ml) chicken broth
1 tbsp salt, or to taste
3 1/2 oz (100 g) Chinese ham

1/2 tsp rice wine
1 tsp cornstarch (cornflour), dissolved in
   1 tbsp water
1/4 tsp MSG

1. Place cauliflower in a pot of cold water and bring to a boil. Blanch 2 minutes and remove, drain, and place in a heat-proof bowl. Add the salt to the chicken broth and pour over the cauliflower. Place the bowl in a steamer and steam the cauliflower until tender. Remove from heat and drain, reserving the broth. Score the cauliflower lengthwise and crosswise, without cutting through to the base. Place it in a serving dish. Keeping it in its original form.
2. Cut the skin off the ham and discard. Place the ham in a heat-proof bowl and add the rice wine. Place the bowl in a steamer and steam for 50 minutes. Remove from heat and chop into small pieces.
3. Pour the reserved chicken broth into a wok and bring to a boil. Add the MSG. Stir the cornstarch to blend and add. Cook, stirring, until thickened and pour over the cauliflower. Sprinkle with the ham and serve.

23. Scrambled Eggs with Pork Slivers, Suzhou Style

2 oz (50 g) lean boneless pork
4 eggs
1/4 tsp salt, or to taste
3 tbsp vegetable oil
1 1/2 tsp rice wine

1 tsp soy sauce
3 1/2 fl oz (100 ml) high stock (see p. 17)
3 tbsp vegetable oil
1/4 tsp MSG

1. Cut the pork into slivers.
2. Beat the eggs until foamy. Add the salt and MSG and mix well.
3. Heat the oil in a wok over medium heat until very hot, about 420°F (220°C), or the oil surface ripples. Add the pork slivers and stir-fry until cooked. Add the eggs and cook until solid. Add the rice wine, soy sauce and stock, stir-fry for 2 to 3 minutes. Remove and serve.

24. Steamed Pork with Spiced Rice Flour, Beijing Style

1 lb (500 g) boneless lean and fat pork with skin
3 tbsp sesame oil
2 1/2 tbsp sugar
5 tsp rice wine
2 1/2 tbsp fermented soya paste

10 tsp scallions, shredded
5 tsp ginger, shredded
1 tbsp five-spice powder
10 tbsp (150 g) spiced rice flour
7 fl oz (200 ml) soy sauce

1. Cut the pork into slices, 2 1/2 inches (6 cm) long and wide and 1/4-inch (6 mm) thick with a piece of skin on each.

2. Mix together the sesame oil, sugar, rice wine, soy sauce, fermented soya paste, five-spice powder, scallions, ginger and marinate for one hour and let the flavours permeate the meat. Mix the spiced rice flour with the pork slices. Stack the pork slices in one large heat-proof bowl or divide them into four individual bowls, with the meat skin side down.

3. Place the bowl or bowls in a steamer and steam for 2 to 3 hours over high heat, adding water as needed, until the meat is very tender. Remove and serve.

25. Five-Spice Flavoured Spareribs, Beijing Style

1 lb (500 g) pork spareribs
3 1/2 tbsp soy sauce
2 cups vegetable oil for deep-frying
2 1/2 tbsp white sugar
1/4 tsp brown sugar
1/2 oz (15 g) scallions, chopped

1 tbsp fresh ginger, chopped
1 tsp rice wine
3 fennel seeds
5 tsp rice vinegar
1 tsp salt, or to taste

1. Wash the spareribs and chop into 1 1/4-inch-long (33 mm) pieces. Soak in cold water to cover for 5 minutes. Remove, drain, and marinate in a little soy sauce for 15 minutes. Drain, dry well, and rub with white sugar, and set aside.
2. Heat the oil in a wok to about 350°F (175°C), or until a piece of scallion green or ginger sizzles and moves around quickly when tossed into the oil. Add the spareribs and deep-fry until golden brown. Remove, drain, and set aside. Pour the oil out of the wok, leaving only enough to cover the bottom.
3. Reheat the wok and add the scallions, ginger, and spareribs. Then add the rice wine, fennel seeds, brown sugar, vinegar and salt and the remaining soy sauce. Stir-fry about 30 seconds. Turn the heat to low and simmer until the sauce thickens and the meat falls from the bones. Remove and serve.

26. Steamed Spareribs, Beijing Style

9 oz (250 g) spareribs
1 1/2 to 2 tbsp beaten whole egg
4 tsp (25 g) dry cornstarch (cornflour)
1 tsp cornstarch dissolved in 2 tsp water
2 cups (500 ml) vegetable oil for deep-frying
1 tbsp scallions, chopped

2 tsp fresh ginger, sliced
2 fennel seeds
7 fl oz (200 ml) pork stock
2 tsp brine
1 tbsp soy sauce
1/2 tsp MSG

1. Wash the spareribs and chop into 1 1/2-inch-long (4 cm) pieces. Mix the beaten egg and the dry cornstarch into a batter and pour it over the spareribs, blending well. Set aside.
2. Heat the oil in a wok over high heat to about 350°F (175°C), or until a piece of scallion green or ginger sizzles and moves around quickly when dropped into the oil. Add the spareribs, one at a time, and deep-fry until golden. Drain and place in a heat-proof bowl. Add brine, soy sauce, rice wine, MSG. Place the scallions, ginger and fennel seeds on top. Place the bowl in a steamer and steam, replenishing the water as needed, until the ribs very tender. Remove from the heat and discard the fennel seeds, scallions and ginger.
3. Place the spareribs in a pot with the stock and heat over high heat until the liquid has reduced by a third. Stir the dissolved cornstarch to blend, and add to the stock. Cook, stirring, until thickened. Remove and serve.

27. Sweet-and-Sour Spareribs, Hangzhou Style

1 1/2 lb (750 g) spareribs
1 tsp rice wine
1/4 tsp salt, or to taste
2 tsp flour
3 tsp dry cornstarch (cornflour)

1 tbsp soy sauce
1 tbsp rice vinegar
2 tbsp sugar
2 cups (500 ml) vegetable oil

1. Chop the spareribs into pieces, 1/2 inch wide by 3/4 inch long (13mm by 20mm). Mix with the rice wine and salt. Mix the cornstarch with 1 tbsp water to make a batter, and pour over the ribs. Stir to coat well.

2. Mix together the soy sauce, rice vinegar, sugar, flour and 4 oz (120 ml) of water to make a sauce. Set aside.

3. Heat the oil in a wok over medium heat to about 230°F (110°C), or until small bubbles appear around a piece of scallion green or ginger tossed into the oil. Add the spareribs and deep-fry until crisp, stirring to keep them from sticking together. Remove and drain well.

4. Reheat the oil to 375°F (190°C), or until a piece of scallion green or ginger sizzles noisily and quickly turns brown. Deep-fry the spareribs until brown golden. Remove and drain. Pour the oil out of the wok. Stir the sauce to blend and pour it into the wok, cook, stirring, until thickened. Add the spareribs and stir until they are covered with sauce. Remove and serve.

28. Pepper-Salt Spareribs, Shanghai Style

3/4 lb (350 g) spareribs
1 tbsp rice wine
1 tbsp soy sauce
2 tbsp cornstarch

4 cups (1 litre) vegetable oil for deep-frying
5 tsp spiced pepper-salt (see p.10)
1/4 tsp MSG

1. Wash the spareribs and chop into pieces, 2 inches long and 3/4 inch wide (5cm by 2cm). Mix the rice wine, soy sauce, MSG, cornstarch, and 2 tsp water into a paste. Add the spareribs and stir to coat well.

2. Heat the oil in a wok over high heat to 350°F (180°C), or until a piece of scallion green or ginger sizzles and moves around quickly when tossed into the oil. Add the spareribs and deep-fry for 1 minute. Remove, drain, and set aside. Reheat the oil to 400°F (205°C), or until a piece of scallion or ginger browns quickly and a haze appears above the oil. Add the spareribs and deep-fry until they are browned and rise to the surface. Remove, drain well, and place in a serving dish. Place two piles of pepper-salt on the edges of the dish as a dip, and serve.

29. Deep-Fried Spring Rolls, Kaifeng-Henan Style

7 oz (200 g) boneless pork, lean and fat
3 oz (100 g) leek
1 tbsp soy sauce
1 tsp brine
2 tsp rice wine
4 tbsp cornstarch (cornflour) dissolved in

4 tbsp water
2 eggs
5 tsp flour
4 cups (1 litre) vegetable oil for deep-frying
1/4 tsp MSG

Filling
1. Cut the pork into thin slices and then along the grain into matchstick-sized slivers. Wash the leeks well and cut into 1 1/2 inch (4 cm) sections. Separate into slices and mix with the pork slivers. Set aside.
2. Heat 4 tbsp of the oil in a wok over high heat to very hot, or until the oil surface ripples. Add the pork slivers, leeks, soy sauce, 1/2 tsp brine, MSG, and rice wine, and stir-fry until the pork is cooked. Stir the cornstarch-water mixture and add 1 tbsp to the wok. Cook, stirring, until the sauce thickens. Remove from the heat and set aside.

Pancakes

1. Beat the eggs and mix with the flour, 1/2 tsp brine, and enough water to make a stiff batter.

2. Heat a pan and add just enough oil to film the surface. Pour in half the batter and rotate the pan so the batter forms a thin pancake. Cook on one side until dry, then turn over and cook the other side just until dry. Repeat with the other half of the batter. Cut each pancake in half and spread a thin layer of the dissolved cornstarch on the upper surface of each (see Illustration I).

Final preparation

1. Place one of the wrappers on a clean surface with the straight edge facing you. Place 1/4 of the pork and leek filling along the straight edge, leaving the farther half of the wrapper clear and leaving space on both sides to roll up the wrapper. Then turn the pancake away from you once so the filling is encased in the wrapper. Fold the 2 side flaps towards the centre (see Illustration II) and continue rolling up the wrapper. Seal with the dissolved cornstarch. Repeat with the other 3 wrappers and the rest of the filling to make 4 spring rolls in all.

2. Heat the oil in a wok over medium heat to 350°F (175°C), or until a piece of scallion green or ginger sizzles and moves around quickly when tossed into the oil. Add the spring rolls to the oil one at a time and deep-fry until reddish-brown. Remove and drain well. Cut each roll into 5 equal portions, stack them in a dish and serve.

30. Steamed Minced Pork with Salted Eggs, Guangdong Style

10 1/2 oz (300 g) boneless lean pork
2 tsp flour
2 salted eggs,' separated
1 tsp sesame oil

5 tsp clear stock (see p. 17)
2 tsp soy sauce
1/4 tsp MSG

1. Mince the pork. Mix in the flour, MSG, the egg whites and sesame oil and blend well. Spread the mixture in a shallow heat-proof dish and pour the egg yolks whole on top of the meat.
2. Place the dish in a steamer and steam over high heat for 8 to 10 minutes, or until the pork is cooked. Pour the clear stock over the pork, sprinkle with the soy sauce, and serve.

'Salted egg: whole egg cured in brine for more than 20 days.

31. Cabbage-Wrapped Pork Rolls, Sichuan Style

9 oz (250 g) boneless pork, lean and fat
1 tsp scallions, chopped
1/2 tsp fresh ginger, chopped
1/4 tsp pepper
4 tbsp cornstarch (cornflour) dissolved in
    4 tbsp water

1 tsp salt, or to taste
9 oz (250 g) Chinese cabbage (*bok choy*)
2 egg whites
2 tsp flour
7 fl oz (200 ml) meat or bone stock
1/4 tsp MSG

1. Mince the pork and mix with the scallions, ginger, ground peppercorn, 3/4 tsp of the salt, and the dissolved cornstarch. Set aside.
2. Trim and discard the tough outer leaves of the cabbage. Wash the tender inner leaves and blanch briefly in boiling water, removing immediately. Drain and let cool.
3. Mix the egg whites and flour into a batter. Spread the inner side of each cabbage leaf thinly with the batter and then the filling. Roll the leaves into cylinders about 1 inch (2 cm) in diameter and seal the openings with the egg batter. Repeat until all the filling has been used.
4. Place the rolls in a heat-proof deep dish or tureen and steam over high heat for 15 minutes. Remove and cool. Cut the rolls into 1 inch (2 cm) sections and steam again until the pork is thoroughly cooked.
5. Heat the stock to boiling. Add the MSG and the remaining 1/4 tsp salt. Pour the stock over the cabbage rolls and serve.

32. Deep-Fried Stuffed Green Peppers, Northeast China Style

9 oz (250 g) green peppers
9 oz (250 g) lean boneless pork
1/2 tsp scallions, chopped
1/2 tsp fresh ginger, chopped
1 tsp salt, or to taste
1 tbsp soy sauce
1/4 tsp five-spice powder

2 eggs, separated
2 tsp flour
1/2 tsp cornstarch (cornflour)
2 cups (500 ml) vegetable oil for deep-frying
1/2 tsp spiced pepper-salt (see p. 10)
1/4 tsp MSG

1. Wash, halve lengthwise, and seed the green peppers. Cut each half into two triangles and dry well. Set aside.
2. For the filling, mince the pork and mix it with the scallions, ginger, salt, soy sauce, five-spice powder, MSG, and half the egg white.
3. Beat the rest of the egg whites with the yolks and mix with the flour, cornstarch and enough water to make a thick batter.
4. Fill the inside of each piece of pepper with the filling level to the edges. And coat the filled side with flour.
5. Heat the oil in a wok over medium heat to 350°F (175°C) or until a piece of scallion green or ginger sizzles and moves about rapidly when tossed into the oil. Dip the filled side of each piece of pepper into the egg batter and then drop it into the oil, filled side down. Deep-fry until the coating is golden brown, then remove, drain well, and place in a dish. Sprinkle with the pepper-salt and serve.

33. Deep-Fried Stuffed Lotus Roots, Shanghai Style

9 oz (250 g) lean boneless pork, minced or
   ground
1 lb (500 g) fresh lotus roots
1 tbsp soy sauce
1 tsp rice wine
1 tsp scallions, chopped
1/2 tsp ginger, chopped

2 eggs, separated
9 oz or 2 1/4 cup (250 g) flour
1 tsp salt, or to taste
2 cups (500 ml) vegetable oil for deep-frying;
   uses about 5 oz (150 ml)
tomato ketchup or Worcestershire sauce
1/4 tsp MSG

1. For the filling, mix the pork with the soy sauce, rice wine, scallions, ginger, MSG and half a beaten egg white. Set aside.
2. Beat the remaining egg white with the yolks and mix with the flour, salt, and enough water to make a thick batter.
3. Cut the lotus roots crosswise into 1/4 inch (5 mm) slices. Divide the filling into portions, and place a filling portion between two slices. Repeat until all the lotus root is used.
4. Heat the oil in a wok to about 350°F (175°C), or until a small piece of scallion green or ginger sizzles and moves about rapidly when tossed into the oil. Dip stuffed lotus roots in the egg batter and add to the oil. Deep-fry until golden brown, remove, and drain. Serve with tomato ketchup or Worcestershire sauce for dipping.

34. Delicacies in Clear Broth, Beijing Style

3 1/2 oz (100 g) cellophane noodles, soaked
1 oz (25 g) dried black Chinese mushrooms, soaked
4 tbsp (60 g) dried shrimps, soaked
2 dried sea cucumbers, reconstituted
2 oz (50 g) fresh tomatoes
3 1/2 oz (100 g) lean boneless pork, minced
2 3/4 tsp salt, or to taste
1 tsp cornstarch (cornflour) dissolved in
  1 tsp water
6 cups (1,500 ml) chicken stock
3 1/2 oz (100 g) dried bamboo shoot slices,
  soaked (or canned sliced bamboo shoots)
1/2 tsp scallions, chopped

2 oz (50 g) Chinese ham
1 tsp sesame oil
1/2 tsp MSG
For egg dumplings:
3 eggs
3 1/2 oz (100 g) pork, minced
1/4 tsp salt
2 tsp soy sauce
1/2 tsp scallions, chopped
1 tsp ginger, chopped
2 tbsp (30 g) dried shrimps, soaked and
  chopped
1/8 tsp MSG

1. Cut the cellophane noodles into 6 inch (15 cm) pieces. Drain the mushrooms, remove the stems, and cut into thin slices. Cut the sea cucumbers into thin slices.
2. Make egg dumplings. (see recipe 71 "Egg Dumplings, Chengdu-Sichuan Style"). Place egg dumplings on a heat-proof dish and steam in a steamer for 10 minutes. Set aside.
3. To make the meatballs, mix the pork with 1/4 tsp of the salt, 1/8 tsp of the MSG, the cornstarch-water mixture, and a little more water. Stir vigorously in the same direction for 1 minute. Form the mixture into small meatballs. Bring the chicken broth to a boil and add the meatballs. Simmer until cooked through and drain, reserving the broth. Set the meatballs aside.
4. Skim any foam from the broth. Add the cellophane noodles, the mushrooms, 2 tbsp shrimps, sea cucumbers, bamboo shoot slices, and 1/2 tsp scallions. Bring to a boil. When the shrimps and mushrooms release their fragrance, add the remaining 2 1/2 tsp of the salt and the remaining 1/4 tsp of the MSG, along with the ham slices, meat balls, egg dumplings, and tomatoes. Return to a boil and remove from the heat. Sprinkle with the sesame oil, and serve.

BEEF AND
MUTTON DISHES

35. Braised Beef with Bamboo Shoots, Chengdu-Sichuan Style

3 1/2 oz (100 g) young bamboo shoots, fresh or canned
2 1/4 lb (1 kg) lean boneless beef
2 tsp ginger, sliced
2 tsp scallions, chopped
10 whole Sichuan peppercorns
1 star anise

1/2 oz (15 g) rock sugar (or substitute 1 tbsp sugar)
4 tbsp (60 ml) vegetable oil
2 tbsp salted fermented soybean
2 tsp salt
3 1/2 tbsp rice wine

1. Soak the bamboo shoots in cold water and cut into small pieces. Blanch quickly in boiling water, drain, and rinse in cold water. Set aside.
2. Cut the beef into 1 inch (3 cm) chunks and place in a pot with cold water to cover. Bring to a boil and skim off the foam. Then add the ginger, scallion, peppercorns, and star anise. Bring back to a boil and add the sugar. Stir until it dissolves. Turn the heat to low and simmer.
3. While the beef is cooking, heat the oil until the surface ripples. Add the soybean paste and stir-fry until it turns slightly red. Add to the beef. When the beef has cooked for about one hour, add the salt, rice wine and the bamboo shoots. Stew the beef another hour until it is very tender, and serve.

36. Tender Stewed Beef, Hangzhou Style

10 1/2 oz (300 g) beef shank
3 1/2 tbsp sugar
5 tsp soy sauce
5 tsp rice wine

1/3 oz (10 g) ground cassia bark
2 tsp fresh ginger, sliced
2 tsp scallions, chopped
3 tbsp sesame oil

1. Remove sinews and tendons from the beef. Blanch for two minutes in boiling water to cover. Remove, drain and rinse under cold water. Cut into chunks.
2. Place a bamboo mat in a casserole. Spread the beef chunks on the mat. Mix together the sugar, soy sauce, rice wine, cassia bark, ginger, scallions, and all but 1 tsp of the sesame oil and pour over the beef. Add water to cover and bring to a boil over high heat. Cover, turn the heat to low and stew for six hours, checking the water level from time to time and adding more warm water if needed. When the beef is fork-tender, place it in a serving dish. Boil the sauce over high heat until thickened. Pour over the beef, sprinkle with the remaining sesame oil and serve.

37. Stewed Beef, Beijing Style

1 lb (500 g) lean boneless beef
2 cups oil for deep frying
1 star anise
5 fl oz (150 g) soy sauce
5 tbsp sugar

1 tsp Sichuan peppercorns
1/3 oz (10 g) stick cinnamon
1 tsp scallions, chopped
2 tsp ginger, sliced

1. Cut the beef into 1 1/2 inches (35mm) chunks. Deep-fry the beef in very hot oil until browned. Drain and set aside.
2. Tie the peppercorns and star anise in a piece of cheesecloth or place in a tea ball.
3. Place 4 cups (1 litre) water in a pot and add the bag of spices, the soy sauce, sugar, stick cinnamon, scallions, and ginger. Bring the water to a boil over high heat and add the beef. Turn the heat to low and stew for 4 hours, or until the beef is very tender and the sauce has cooked down almost completely, but without scorching.

38. Curried Beef, Guangdong Style

14 oz (400 g) lean boneless beef
3 cups (750 ml) vegetable oil for deep-frying;
  uses about 2 1/2 oz (75 ml)
2 tbsp curry oil
1/4 tsp ginger, chopped
1/4 tsp garlic, chopped
1/4 tsp onions, chopped
1/4 tsp hot red chili (chilli) pepper, chopped

2 tsp rice wine
2 oz (60 ml) clear stock
1/4 tsp salt, or to taste
1/2 tsp sugar
1 tsp cornstarch (cornflour) dissolved in 1
  tsp water
1/4 tsp MSG

1. Cut beef into 1-inch square chunks.
2. Heat the oil in a wok over low heat to very hot, 350°F (180°C). Deep-fry the beef until it is cooked through. Remove beef, drain, and set aside.
3. Pour the oil out of the wok, leaving a thin film on the bottom. Reheat until a haze appears on the oil surface. Add the curry oil, ginger, garlic, onions, chili pepper, rice wine, stock, salt, MSG and sugar. Stir the cornstarch to blend and add. Add the beef, stir-fry for 2 minutes, or until the sauce is thickened. Sprinkle with sesame oil and serve.

39. Braised Beef, Shanxi Style

1 lb (400 g) lean boneless beef
10 tsp (50 ml) soy sauce
4 tbsp cornstarch (cornflour), dissolved in
   4 tbsp water
3 oz (100 g) scallions, chopped
3 1/2 fl oz (100 ml) sesame oil

1/2 g fennel seed
3 1/2 oz (100 ml) chicken or duck broth
2 tsp rice wine
1/4 tsp fresh ginger, chopped
1/4 tsp MSG

1. Wash the beef and cut into thin slices. Mix with the soy sauce and scallions. Stir the cornstarch-water mixture and add.

2. Heat the sesame oil in a wok and add the fennel seeds. Heat to very hot or until the oil starts to smoke, and add the beef. Stir-fry until barely cooked. Add the stock, rice wine and MSG. Cover the wok, and boil rapidly for 1 minute. Add the ginger, stir and remove.

40. Boiled Beef, Sichuan Style

9 oz (250 g) lean boneless beef
3 oz (100 g) asparagus lettuce (substitute asparagus)
5 dried hot red chili (chilli) peppers
1/2 tsp salt, or to taste
2 tbsp cornstarch (cornflour) dissolved in 2 tbsp water
5 tsp hot and salted fermented soybean paste

5 tsp sweet fermented glutinous rice wine (or rice wine)
4 1/2 oz (125 ml) vegetable oil
20 whole Sichuan peppercorns
3 oz (100 g) scallions, chopped into 2 inches long sections
2 cups (500 ml) beef stock
1 tsp chili (chilli) oil

1. Wash the beef and cut into slices 2 inches long by 1 inch wide and 1/8 inch thick (5 cm by 25 mm by 4 mm). Slice the asparagus. Seed and chop the chili peppers.
2. Place beef in a bowl and add the salt, cornstarch-water mixture, soy sauce, soybean paste (chopped) and rice wine. Mix well.
3. Heat the oil in a wok over low heat to about 230°F (110°C), or until bubbles appear around a small piece of scallion green or ginger tossed into the oil. Add the chopped chili pepper and deep-fry until purplish-red. Add the peppercorns, scallions, and asparagus, and stir-fry for 1 minute. Add the stock and bring to a boil. Add the beef, stirring with a wok scoop to keep them separate. Boil the beef until it turns shiny. Remove, sprinkle with the chili oil, and serve.

41. Sesame Beef Filet, Northeast China Style

17 oz (500 g) beef filet
5 tsp salt, or to taste
2 eggs
1/2 cup (120 ml) flour

1/2 cup (120 ml) whole sesame seeds
2 cups (500 ml) vegetable oil for deep-frying
2 tsp chili (chilli) oil
1/2 tsp MSG

1. Wash the beef and cut into 1/4 inch (5 mm) slices. Mix with the salt and MSG and set aside.
2. Beat the eggs. Dip the beef slices in the flour and then into the egg. Coat with the sesame seeds, pressing them into the beef with your palm or a rolling pin.
3. Heat the oil in a wok to about 350°F (170°C), or until a small piece of scallion green or ginger sizzles and moves around rapidly when tossed into the oil. Add the beef and deep-fry for 2 minutes. Turn and continue to fry for another minute, or until the coating turns golden. Remove and drain. Serve with a small dish of the chili oil as a dip.

42. Beef with Satin Eggs, Guangdong Style

10 1/2 oz (300 g) boneless veal or beef sirloin
5 eggs
1/4 tsp salt
1/8 tsp pepper
1/4 tsp scallions, chopped
1/4 tsp ginger, chopped
2 tsp meat broth seasoned with salt, sugar,

sesame oil and pepper to taste
1/2 tsp cornstarch (cornflour) dissolved in
1/2 tsp water
2 cups (500 ml) vegetable oil for deep-frying;
uses about 3 1/2 oz (100 ml)
3/4 tsp MSG

1. Wash the beef and cut into 1 inch (3 cm) chunks.
2. Beat the eggs and mix in the salt, MSG, pepper and scallion.
3. Heat the oil in a wok. Deep-fry the beef over a low fire until cooked. Remove and drain well.
4. Pour the oil out of the wok, leaving only enough to cover the bottom, about 3 tbsp. Heat until the oil surface ripples. Add the ginger, beef, and broth. Bring to a boil. Stir the cornstarch-water mixture and add. Stirring, to make a thin gravy. Sprinkle with the sesame oil. Add the eggs and cook, stirring, until they are scrambled but still soft. Remove and serve.

43. Sautéed Beef Strips, Jilin Style

1 lb (500 g) beef filet or boneless sirloin
2 tsp salt, or to taste
1 tbsp soy sauce
1/2 tsp fresh ginger, chopped
1/2 tsp sesame oil
5-6 scallions, white parts only
1/4 tsp powdered hot red chili
1/4 tsp vinegar

1/2 tsp ginger, chopped
1/2 tsp garlic, chopped
1 tsp ground roasted sesame seed
2 eggs
3 tsp flour
2 cups (500 ml) vegetable oil for deep-frying
1/2 tsp MSG

1. Wash beef and cut into 2 by 1 by 1/8 inch (60mm by 30mm by 3 mm) slices. Marinate with the salt, 1 tsp of the soy sauce, the ginger, 1/4 tsp of the MSG, and the sesame oil for 10 minutes.
2. Cut the scallions in half crosswise, then quarter each lengthwise into four strips. Set aside.
3. Make a dipping sauce by mixing together the remaining 2 tsp soy sauce and 1/4 tsp MSG, the chili powder, vinegar, ginger, garlic, and the sesame seed.
4. Beat the eggs. Add the flour and enough water to make a paste.
5. String the beef strips and scallions, alternating, on bamboo or metal skewers. Coat with the egg paste.
6. Heat the oil in a pan to moderately hot, about 230°F (110°C). Shallow-fry the beef on both sides until golden-brown. Remove, drain, and serve with the sauce.

44. Braised Beef and Potatoes, Northeast China Style

17 oz (500 g) lean boneless beef sirloin
1/2 lb (250 g) potatoes
1 large carrot
2 cups (500 ml) water
1 tbsp coriander, chopped
1/2 tsp scallions, shredded

1/4 tsp fresh ginger, chopped
1/4 tsp ground Sichuan peppercorns
5 tsp vegetable oil
1 tbsp soy sauce
2 tsp salt, or to taste

1. Wash the beef and cut into 1 inch (30 mm) chunks. Place in a pot of cold water to cover and bring to a boil. Let boil 1 minute, then remove and drain the beef and set aside.
2. Peel and wash the potatoes and cut into triangles or chunks the same size as the beef. Peel the carrot and dice or cut into small slices.
3. Heat the water in a wok, or a pot or a casserole, and add the scallions, ginger, and ground peppercorn. Add the beef chunks and vegetable oil, and bring to a boil. Reduce the heat to a slow simmer. Cover and simmer for 1 hour, or until the beef is cooked but not fork-tender. Add the potatoes, carrots, soy sauce, and salt. Continue simmering until the beef is tender, checking the water and replenishing if necessary. If excess water remains when the beef is cooked, reduce to the desired amount by boiling over high heat. Add the MSG and sprinkle the coriander over the beef and serve.

45. Stewed Beef Strips, Shandong Style

1 3/4 lb (750 g) lean boneless beef sirloin
3 tbsp scallions, chopped in sections
1 tsp ginger, sliced
4 tbsp (60 ml) soy sauce
1 tsp salt, or to taste

5 tsp rice wine
3 cloves star anise
1 tbsp cornstarch, dissolved in 1 tbsp water
5 tsp sesame oil

1. Soak the beef in cool water for 15 minutes. Wash off any blood. Cook in boiling water to cover 10 minutes. Remove, rinse, and drain.
2. Place in a pot with 4 cups (1 litre) of water, half the scallions, and 1/4 tsp of the sliced ginger. Bring to a boil over high heat and skim off the foam. Cover tightly and reduce the heat to a low simmer. Cook for 2 to 3 hours, replenishing the water if needed. When the beef is fork-tender, drain, reserving the cooking liquid. Let the meat cool enough to be handled, then trim the edges, discarding any fat and membranes. Cut across the grain into slices 3 inches long by 1 inch wide and 1/4 inch thick (8 cm by 3 cm by 5 mm).
3. Stack in a heat-proof bowl, and add 2 tbsp of the soy sauce, salt, rice wine, the rest of the scallions and ginger, the star anise, and the reserved cooking liquid. Place the bowl in a steamer and steam for 20 minutes. Place the beef in a serving dish and pour the stock into a wok. Heat the stock and add the remaining 2 tbsp of soy sauce. When it comes to a boil, stir the cornstarch-water mixture and add. Cook, stirring, until thickened, and sprinkle with sesame oil. Pour the sauce over the beef and serve.

46. Stir-Fried Milk, Guangdong Style

3 1/2 oz (100 g) shrimps, shelled
3 1/2 oz (100 g) chicken livers, diced
11 egg whites
1/4 tsp salt, or to taste
2 tbsp water chestnut flour (substitute cornstarch)
10 tbsp (150 ml) vegetable oil for deep-frying
14 oz (400 ml) milk

2 tsp (10 g) Chinese ham, steamed and diced
1 oz (25 g) olive nuts, deep-fried
marinade:
1/2 egg white
1/4 tsp salt, or to taste
1/4 tsp cornstarch (cornflour)
1/4 tsp baking soda
1/8 tsp MSG

1. Beat 11 egg whites. Add salt and water chestnut flour into milk. Stir in egg white and mix well.
2. Mix the shrimps with the marinade and let stand. Cook the chicken liver in boiling water until barely cooked, remove and drain.
3. Heat 4 tbsp of the vegetable oil in a wok over medium heat to 210°F (100°C), or until small bubbles appear around a piece of scallion green or ginger tossed into the oil. Add the shrimps and chicken liver, and fry just long enough to seal in the juices. Remove and drain well.
4. Heat 6 tbsp oil in the wok over low heat to just warm. Gradually add the milk, stirring in only one direction until the milk thickens. Add the shrimps, chicken livers, and ham. Cook, stirring until the milk is cooked. Remove in a dish. Sprinkle with the deep-fried olive nuts, and serve.

47. Simmered Oxtail, Inner Mongolian Style

1 lb (500 g) oxtail
4 tbsp (60 ml) vegetable oil
2 cloves star anise
1/2 tsp scallions, shredded
1/2 tsp fresh ginger, shredded
1/2 tsp garlic, sliced

1 tsp sweet soybean paste
4 tsp soy sauce
1/2 tsp sugar
6 cups (1,500 ml) beef stock
1/4 tsp sesame oil
1/4 tsp MSG

1. Wash the oxtail and cut crosswise through the joints of the bone. Boil in water to cover until tender. Remove and drain.

2. Heat the oil in a wok to very hot, or until the oil surface ripples. Add the star anise and fry until fragrant. Discard the star anise and add the scallions, ginger, and garlic. Stir-fry until fragrant, and stir in the sweet soy bean paste. Add the soy sauce, sugar, stock and oxtail and bring to a boil. Simmer over low heat until the stock thickens. Add the MSG and sprinkle with the sesame oil. Remove and serve.

48. Deep-Fried Mutton, Kaifeng Style

7 oz (200 g) cooked mutton
2 tsp salt water
2 tsp rice wine
1 1/2 beaten eggs

3 tbsp flour
1 tbsp cornstarch (cornflour)
2 cups (500 ml) vegetable oil
Spiced pepper-salt (see p. 10) for the dip

1. Cut the mutton into 3/4 inch (2 cm) chunks. Mix with the salt water and rice wine and let marinate for several hours. Remove and dry.

2. Mix the beaten egg, flour, cornflour and enough salt water to make a batter. Stir in 1 tbsp of the oil. Coat mutton chunks with the batter.

3. Heat the remaining oil in a wok over high heat to very hot, about 350°F (180°C). Add the mutton chunks and deep-fry until brown. Remove and drain. Sprinkle with the spiced pepper-salt.

49. Mongolian Hot Pot, Beijing Style

1 lb (500 g) lean boneless leg of lamb
lamb tail fat, sliced
ginger slices
scallion slices
soy sauce
For the dips
sesame paste
fermented bean curd
shrimp oil

soy sauce
vinegar
rice wine
preserved Chinese chive flowers
preserved sweet garlic
Chinese coriander, chopped (or cilantro)
chili (chilli) oil
Cooking utensil: a charcoal-burning fire pot
    for cooking at the table.

1. Cut the mutton into paper-thin slices about 2 1/2 inches by 1 inch (6 cm by 3 cm). It will be easier to slice if partially frozen first. Spread them on individual serving dishes. Arrange the dips and side dishes in bowls.

2. Half-fill the fire pot with boiling water. Add the sliced scallion and ginger, mutton tail fat, and a little soy sauce. Cover the pot lid tightly. Fill the chimney with burning charcoal and bring the stock to a boil.

3. To eat, the diners mix their own sauces from the condiments and seasonings. Then they pick up the mutton slices and cook them in the boiling stock for a few seconds, until the meat turns pinkish-white. The meat is then dipped into the sauce. The best pastry to go with the meat is *shaobing* —the Chinese baked sesame cakes.

Note: If you do not own a Chinese fire pot, use a saucepan on a hot plate, or an electric wok.

50. Stewed Mutton Slices, Northeast China Style

1 lb (500 g) cooked mutton
4 tbsp (60 ml) vegetable oil
3 cloves star anise
1/2 tsp scallions, chopped
1/2 tsp fresh ginger, chopped
2 tsp sweet soybean paste

2 tsp soy sauce
2 tsp salt, or to taste
1/2 tsp sugar
1/4 tsp peppercorn oil
1/4 tsp MSG

1. Cut mutton into 2 1/2 inch by 1 1/4 inch by 1/2 inch (6 cm by 3 cm by 5 mm) slices.
2. Heat oil in a wok over high heat until smoke rises. Add star anise to deep-fry until fragrant. Remove star anise and discard. Add scallions and ginger to stir-fry until fragrant. Stir in sweet bean sauce and stir swiftly until its aroma releases. Add mutton strips, soy sauce, salt, sugar and water to level with the meat. Bring sauce to a boil, skim the foam and cover wok with a lid. Turn the heat to a low simmer, cook until the meat tender. You may consume the excess sauce by boiling over a high fire until the sauce thickens. Add MSG. Sprinkle with peppercorn oil. Remove and serve.

51. Crisp-Fried Mutton, Northeast China Style

9 oz (250 g) raw mutton, minced
9 oz (250 g) cooked mutton, minced
2 eggs, lightly beaten
2 tsp salt
2 tsp soy sauce
1/2 tsp scallions, chopped

1/2 tsp ginger, chopped
1/4 tsp sesame oil
4 tsp cornstarch (cornflour)
2 cups (500 ml) vegetable oil for deep-frying
spiced pepper-salt (see p. 10)
1/4 tsp MSG

1. Mix together the minced mutton, eggs, salt, soy sauce, scallions, ginger, sesame oil, MSG, and cornstarch. Stir vigorously in one direction for 2 minutes, or until stiff. Shape into oval balls and roll in cornstarch. Flatten the balls slightly and make criss-cross marks on top.
2. Heat the oil in a wok to about 350°F (175°C), or until a piece of scallion green or ginger sizzles and moves about rapidly when dropped into the oil. Add the mutton balls and deep-fry until brown. Remove, drain, and cut into strips. Sprinkle with the spiced pepper-salt and serve.

52. Peppery-Hot Mutton, Northeast China Style

1 lb (500 g) cooked mutton
2 dried hot red chili (chilli) peppers
3 1/2 oz (100 ml) vegetable oil
1/2 tsp scallions, sliced diagonally
1/2 tsp vinegar
2 tsp salt

1 tbsp soy sauce
bone stock
1/4 tsp ground Sichuan peppercorns
1/4 tsp sesame oil
1/4 tsp MSG

1. Slice mutton. Halve, seed, wash, and dice the chili peppers.
2. Heat the oil in a wok to very hot, or until the oil surface ripples. Add the mutton slices and fry for 30 seconds. Remove and drain.
3. Pour the oil out of the wok, leaving only enough to cover the bottom. Reheat and add the scallions and chili peppers, stir-frying until fragrant. Add the mutton and stir in the vinegar, salt, soy sauce, and enough stock to cover the mutton about half-way. Sprinkle with the ground peppercorn and bring to a boil. Turn the fire to low and simmer until the sauce thickens. Add MSG. Sprinkle with sesame oil, remove, and serve.

53. Roast Mutton Kebabs,
Xinjiang-Inner Mongolian Style

1 lb (500 g) lean boneless mutton
2 tsp salt
1/2 tsp pepper
2 tsp soy sauce
1/4 tsp scallions, chopped

1/4 tsp fresh ginger, chopped
1/2 tsp peppercorn water
1/2 tsp sesame oil
1/4 tsp MSG

1. Slice the mutton very thinly. Mix together the salt, pepper, soy sauce, scallion, ginger, peppercorn water, MSG, and sesame oil, add to the mutton, stirring until well-coated. Let marinate 30 minutes or longer.
2. String the mutton slices on skewers. Roast over a charcoal fire until cooked through, and serve.

54. Slivered Mutton with Young Ginger, Sichuan Style

7 oz (200 g) lean boneless mutton
2 tsp rice wine
1/2 tsp salt
2 oz (50 g) young ginger
1 medium green pepper, halved and seeded
1 tsp dissolved cornstarch (cornflour) dissolved in 1 tsp water

2 tsp soy sauce
5 tbsp vegetable oil
1 oz (35 g) garlic shoots (substitute 1 tbsp sliced garlic)
1 tsp sweet bean sauce (made from fermented flour, can be substituted with Hoisin sauce)

1. Cut the mutton into fine slivers and mix with the rice wine and salt. Cut the tender ginger and green pepper into slivers.
2. Mix together the cornstarch-water and soy sauce. Set aside.
3. Heat the oil in a wok to very hot, or until the oil surface ripples. Add the green pepper and stir-fry until they start to wilt. Remove and drain. Add the mutton slivers and stir-fry a few moments. Add the ginger, green pepper, and garlic shoots. Stir-fry several times. Stir in the sweet bean sauce. Stir the cornstarch sauce and add. Cook, stirring until thickened. Remove and serve.

55. Deep-Fried Beef or Mutton Rolls, Northeast-Northwest Style

1 lb (500 g) lean boneless beef or mutton
4 tsp salt
1/4 tsp ground Sichuan peppercorns
1/2 tsp scallions, chopped
1/2 tsp fresh ginger, chopped
2 tsp cornstarch (cornflour)

3 tsp flour
3 dried bean-curd sheets
2 cups (500 ml) vegetable oil for deep-frying
1/4 tsp spiced pepper-salt (see p. 10)
1/4 tsp MSG

1. For the filling, mince the meat and mix with the salt, ground peppercorns, scallions, ginger, 1/4 tsp of the cornstarch, the MSG, and enough water to bind the ingredients together. Set aside.
2. Mix the other 1/4 tsp of cornstarch with the flour and enough water to make a thick paste.
3. Soak the bean-curd sheets in warm water until soft. Take 1 sheet and spread the paste on the upper surface. Spread 1/3 of the meat filling lengthwise down the centre, leaving room at the bottom and on both sides. Fold up the bottom flap and start rolling. Midway, fold the two side flaps towards the

centre. Continue rolling (see Illustration I). Seal the open end with a dab of flour paste. Repeat with the other two rolls.

4. Place the rolls on a heat-proof dish and place in a steamer. Steam until the meat is cooked. Remove the rolls. Wrap each tightly in a piece of clean cheesecloth. Let stand until cool, then unwrap and cut crosswise into 1-inch or 30 mm long sections.

5. Heat the oil in a wok over medium heat to 400°F (205°C), or until a piece of scallion green or ginger quickly turns brown when tossed into the oil and a haze appears above the surface. Add the rolls and deep-fry until reddish-brown. Remove and drain well. Sprinkle with the spiced pepper-salt and serve.

56. Stir-Fried Lamb Kidney, Liver and Filet, Beijing-Hebei Style

3 1/2 oz (100 g) lamb kidney
3 1/2 oz (100 g) lamb liver
3 1/2 oz (100 g) lamb filet
5 tsp dry cornstarch (cornflour)
5 tsp soy sauce
2 tsp rice wine
1 tsp vinegar

3 1/2 tbsp (50 ml) lamb bone stock
2 cups (500 ml) vegetable oil for deep-frying;
   uses about 2 1/2 oz (75 ml)
1 tsp scallions, chopped
1 tsp fresh ginger, chopped
1/4 tsp MSG

1. Skin the kidney and slice it in half. Cut out the white and dark-red parts and cut into 1/8-inch thin slices. Slice the liver and filet into pieces the same size as the kidney and mix well with the dry cornstarch. Set aside.
2. Mix the soy sauce, rice wine, vinegar, dissolved cornstarch, stock, and MSG into a sauce. Set aside.
3. Heat the oil in a wok to 400°F (205°C), or until a piece of scallion green or ginger browns quickly when tossed into the oil and a haze appears above the surface. Add the meats and stir-fry for 1 to 2 minutes. Remove and drain. Pour the oil out of the wok, leaving only enough to cover the bottom. Reheat and add the scallions and ginger. Stir-fry until fragrant and add the meat slices. Then stir the sauce and add to the wok. Stir-fry about 1 minute, or until the sauce thickens. Remove and serve.

POULTRY AND

EGG DISHES

57. Yuexiu Chicken, Guangdong Style

1 whole small fryer chicken, pullet or capon, about 2 1/4 lb (1 kg)
5 tsp powdered ginger

1 tbsp salt, or to taste
4 cups (1 litre) sesame oil
1 cup clear stock

1. Wash the chicken. Mix the ginger and salt, and rub over the chicken, inside and out. Let marinate for 1 hour.

2. Pour the sesame oil into a wok and add the stock, boil over high heat for 15 minutes. Add the chicken breast side up, and deep-fry for 15 minutes. Carefully turn the chicken over and boil for 5 more minutes, or until cooked through.

3. Remove the chicken and drain well. Cut into 1 1/2 inch (4 cm) chunks. Pour off the oil, which will float on top of the stock. Pour the stock over the chicken and serve.

58. Steamed Chicken, Shandong Style

1 whole chicken, about 2 1/2 lb (1 kg)
4 tsp salt, or to taste
5 oz (150 g) scallions, chopped
5 tsp (25 g) fresh ginger, shredded
1/4 tsp (2 g) cloves

1/4 tsp (1 g) fennel seed
1/4 tsp (1 g) Dahurian angelica root, chopped, if available
1/2 tsp whole Sichuan peppercorn
3 1/2 tbsp rice wine

1. Wash the chicken. Mix together the salt, half the scallions, and half the ginger, and rub over the chicken inside and out. Mix together the remaining scallions and ginger, the cloves, fennel seed, angelica, ground peppercorns, and rice wine, and place in the chicken cavity.
2. Place the chicken on a heat-proof dish in a steamer and steam for 1 1/2 hours. Remove from the heat and let cool. Discard the seasonings in the body cavity.
3. Chop the chicken into 1 inch by 2 inch (5 cm by 3 cm) chunks and serve.

59. Stewed Chicken with Oyster Sauce, Guangdong Style

1 whole fryer chicken or capon, about 3 1/4 lb
2 tsp soy sauce
2 tsp rice wine
4 cups (1 litre) vegetable oil for deep-frying
1 oz (25 g) dried Chinese black mushrooms, soaked and sliced
2 oz (50 g) bamboo shoots, sliced
3 tbsp scallions, chopped
5 tsp fresh ginger, sliced
2 oz (50 g) Yunnan preserved vegetable (a

  kind of salted mustard), sliced
1 oz (25 g) dates
2 cups (500 ml) chicken stock
2 tbsp oyster sauce
2 1/2 tbsp sugar
1 tsp salt, or to taste
1/4 tsp ground Sichuan peppercorn
2 tbsp cornstarch dissolved in 2 tbsp water
1/4 tsp sesame oil
2 tsp MSG

1. Mix soy sauce and rice wine and rub over the chicken inside and out. Heat the oil in a wok to 230°F (110°C). Add the chicken and deep-fry until brown. Remove and drain. Pour the oil out of the wok.
2. Blanch the mushrooms and bamboo shoot slices briefly in boiling water, drain, and set aside.
3. Pour 3 1/2 oz (100 ml) of oil back into the wok over high heat to 340°F (170°C) until the surface ripples. Add the scallions and ginger and stir-fry. Add the remaining rice wine, soy sauce, mushrooms, bamboo shoots, preserved vegetable, dates, stock, oyster sauce, sugar, salt, peppercorn and chicken. Boil, then reduce heat to low and simmer chicken until cooked. Add MSG.
4. Remove mushrooms, bamboo shoots, and dates, and place in serving dish. Remove chicken, chop into 1 by 2 inch (3 cm by 5 cm) chunks, and stack in the serving dish. Discard preserved vegetable. Stir cornstarch-water mixture, add to the wok, stirring, until thick. Pour over the chicken and serve.

60. Piquant Chicken, Sichuan Style

1 whole fryer chicken or capon, about 2 lb (1,000 g)
2 tbsp soy sauce
1 tsp vinegar
1 tsp scallions, chopped
1 tsp fresh ginger, chopped

1 tsp chili (chilli) oil
1/2 tsp sesame oil
1/2 tsp pepper
1/2 tsp ground Sichuan peppercorn
1 tbsp sugar
1/2 tsp MSG

1. Wash the chicken and place in a pot of boiling water to cover. Boil over high heat for 30 minutes, remove, drain, and let cool. Chop into 1 1/2 inch by 2 inch (4cm X 5cm) pieces and place in a serving dish.
2. Mix all the seasonings together until the sugar is dissolved. Pour over the chicken and serve.
Note: This dish is known for its combination of piquant, peppery-hot flavours, hence the Chinese name "Piquant Chicken."

61. Stewed Chicken Drumsticks, Beijing-Hebei Style

5 oz (150 g) chicken drumstick meat
3 tbsp scallion oil (see below)
7 oz (200 ml) high stock (see p. 17)
1 tsp salt, or to taste

1 tsp rice wine
5 tsp soy sauce
7 tsp cornstarch (cornflour)
1/4 tsp MSG

1. Make the scallion oil by cooking 2 tbsp chopped scallions in 3 tbsp oil until the scallions becomes fragrant. Discard the scallions and set the oil aside.
2. Cut the drumstick meat into 1 1/2 inch chunks.
3. Pour the stock into a wok and stir in the salt, MSG, rice wine, and soy sauce. Bring to a boil and add the chicken pieces, skin side down. Simmer over medium heat, until the sauce has reduced by about 2/3, and the meat becomes tender.
4. Stir the cornstarch-water mixture and add to the wok. Cook, stirring, until thickened. Pour the scallion oil over all, and serve.

62. Bang Bang Chicken, Sichuan Style

9 oz (250 g) chicken breasts and thighs
1 tsp scallions, shredded
1 tsp sesame paste
2 tsp chili (chilli) oil
1 tsp sugar

1 tbsp mushroom soy sauce (or substitute superior soy sauce)
1/8 tsp ground Sichuan peppercorn
1/2 tsp sesame oil
1/4 tsp MSG

1. Poach the chicken in boiling water to cover for 10 minutes, or until cooked. Remove, drain, and let cool. Beat the skin side lightly to loosen the fibres with a *bang* (in Chinese, a wooden stick) or a wooden rolling pin. Peel off the skin and tear the meat into long strips with your fingers. You may cut the skin into strips also. Arrange the chicken strips in a dish and sprinkle with the scallions shreds.
2. Mix together the sesame paste, chili oil, sugar, soy sauce, MSG, ground peppercorns and sesame oil. Pour over the scallions and chicken and mix until coated and serve.

63. Braised Chicken, Suzhou Style

9 oz (250 g) boned chicken
1 medium Chinese yam or potato, about 5 oz (150 g), parboiled
2 cups (500 ml) vegetable oil for deep-frying
1 tbsp rice wine
3 tbsp soy sauce

1/4 tsp salt, or to taste
1 tbsp sugar
1 tbsp cornstarch (cornflour), dissolved in 1 tbsp water
1 cup (200 ml) high stock (see p. 17)
2 tsp sesame oil

1. Wash the chicken and chop into 1 1/2 inch (4 cm) pieces. Peel the yam or potatoes and roll-cut diagonally into 1 1/2 inch (4 cm) pieces.
2. Heat the oil in a wok to 375° F (190°C), or until a piece of scallion green or ginger sizzles noisily and browns quickly when tossed into the oil. Add the chicken and deep-fry to a turn of colour. Remove the chicken and drain. Pour the oil out of the wok, leaving about 2 tbsp. Put the chicken back into the wok and add the rice wine. Simmer over medium heat for 20 minutes. Add the soy sauce, sugar, yam and stock and continue simmering, until the chicken is tender.
3. If too much liquid is left in the wok, reduce by boiling rapidly. Stir the dissolved cornstarch and add to the wok. Cook, stirring, until the sauce thickens. Sprinkle with the sesame oil, and serve.

64. Creamy Curried Chicken, Guangdong Style

1 1/2 lb (750 g) chicken, whole or pieces
2 medium potatoes, about 9 oz (250 g), peeled
4 cups (1 litre) vegetable oil for deep-frying
2 cups (500 ml) chicken stock
1 1/2 tsp salt, or to taste
4 1/2 tsp sugar
3 dried hot red chili (chilli) peppers, seeded
  and chopped

1 tbsp fresh ginger, chopped
7 tbsp (100 g) onions, chopped
2 tbsp curry oil
3 tbsp flour
2 1/2 fl oz coconut milk
3 1/2 fl oz (100 ml) milk
1/4 tsp MSG

1. Wash the chicken and chop into 1 1/2 inch (4 cm) pieces. Roll-cut the potatoes into pieces the same size.
2. Heat the oil in a wok to 350°F (180°C), or very hot. Add the chicken and deep-fry until cooked. Remove, drain, set aside. Deep-fry the potatoes until cooked through but not browned, remove, drain well, and set aside. Pour the hot oil out of the wok leaving only enough to cover the bottom. Add the rice wine, chicken stock, salt, sugar, MSG, potatoes and chicken and let come to a boil.
3. In the meantime, heat 5 oz (150 ml) of oil in another wok, and add the hot chili peppers, ginger, onion, and curry oil. Stir-fry until fragrant, then pour into the other wok.
4. Put the potato and chicken pieces in a large heat-proof bowl, cover with the stock, and place in a steamer to steam until the chicken is very tender.
5. Heat 1 tbsp oil in the wok and stir in the flour to make a paste, taking care not to burn it.
6. Place the potatoes in a serving dish. Arrange the chicken pieces on top. Strain the stock and discard the solids. Add the coconut milk and milk to the stock. Add the flour paste to the stock and simmer, stirring, until thickened and the flour loses its raw taste. Pour over chicken and serve.

65. Braised Chicken with Chestnuts, Beijing-Hebei Style

1 lb (500 g) chicken pieces
1 1/2 tsp scallions, chopped
5 oz (150 g) chestnuts
1 1/2 tsp fresh ginger, chopped
1 tsp rice wine

2 cloves star anise
5 tbsp vegetable oil
4 tbsp sugar
8 tsp soy sauce
1/2 tsp MSG

1. Wash the chicken and place in a heat-proof bowl. Add 1 tsp scallion, 1 tsp ginger, rice wine, and star anise. Put the bowl in a steamer and steam for 30 minutes. Remove the chicken, drain, let cool, and chop into 1 1/2 inch (4cm) pieces. Reserve the liquid in the bowl.
2. While the chicken steams, make a cross in the shell of each chestnut and place in a saucepan with water to cover. Bring to a boil and boil for 3 to 5 minutes. Remove from the heat and let cool in the water. Shell and peel, but leave whole.
3. Heat the oil in a wok over high heat until the surface ripples. Add the chestnuts and stir-fry for 10 minutes. Drain and set aside.
4. Add the sugar to the wok and stir until melted. Add 1/2 tsp scallions, 1/2 tsp ginger, and chicken, and stir-fry until the chicken skin browns. Then add the soy sauce. Continue to stir-fry for about 1 minute and add the chestnuts. Pour in the chicken liquid, bring to a boil, and simmer over medium heat for 20 minutes. Remove and serve.

66. Crisp-Fried Duck, Shanxi Style

1 duck, about 5 1/2 lb (2,500 g)
4 tbsp rice wine
3 1/2 fl oz (100 ml) soy sauce
1/2 tsp salt, or to taste
5 tsp ground Sichuan peppercorn
1 tsp ground star anise
2 tbsp sweet bean sauce (fermented flour sauce)

5 tsp scallions, shredded
1 tbsp fresh ginger, shredded
1/2 tsp ground clove
1/2 tsp ground cinnamon
10 cups (2,500 ml) vegetable oil for deep-frying; uses about 5 oz (150 ml)
2 tbsp spiced pepper-salt (see p. 10)

1. Wash the duck. Mix together the rice wine, soy sauce, salt, ground peppercorns, ground star anise, sweet bean sauce, scallions, ginger, ground clove, and cinnamon. Rub the duck with the mixture inside and out and let marinate for 4 hours.
2. Place the duck in a heat-proof dish and steam in a steamer over high heat for 4 hours, replenishing the water as needed. Remove the duck and drain.
3. Heat the oil in a wok over high heat to 400°F (200°C), or until a piece of scallion green or ginger browns quickly when tossed into the oil or a haze appears above the oil surface. Carefully add the duck, breast-side down, and deep-fry until brown. Carefully turn the duck over and deep-fry the other side until brown. Remove, drain thoroughly, and chop into 1 1/2 inch (4cm) pieces. Serve with the spiced pepper-salt as a dip.

67. Stir-Fried Chicken Cubes with Scallions and Peppercorns, Kaifeng-Henan Style

9 oz (250 g) boned chicken
1 tsp roasted Sichuan peppercorns
1 tsp scallion sections
1 tsp rice wine
1 tsp scallions, shredded
4 tbsp cornstarch (cornflour)
1 egg

1 tbsp soy sauce
2 cups (500 ml) vegetable oil for deep-frying
1 tsp ginger, shredded
1 tsp salt water (brine)
2 tbsp sesame oil
1/2 tsp MSG

1. Skin the chicken, and cut it into 1/2 inch by 1 inch (13mm by 20mm) cubes. Set aside.
2. Soak the peppercorns in the rice wine until soft, then remove from rice wine and mix with the scallions and chop very finely.
3. Mix the cornstarch, egg, and 1 tsp of the soy sauce into a thick batter. Add the chicken cubes and stir to coat well.
4. Heat the oil in a wok over high heat to 225°F (110°C), or small bubbles appear around a piece of scallion tossed into the oil. Add the chicken cubes and cook, stirring with chopsticks to separate, for

1 to 1 1/2 minutes, or until the cubes shrink slightly and turn lighter in colour. Remove, drain well, and set aside.

5. Pour the oil out of the wok, leaving only enough to cover the bottom. Reheat over high heat until the oil surface ripples. Then add the scallion-and-peppercorn mixture, the shredded scallions, and the ginger shreds. Splash in the reserved rice wine, salt water, the remaining 2 tsp of soy sauce, the MSG, and the chicken. Stir-fry about 1 minute, until blended. Remove, sprinkle with the sesame oil, and serve.

68. Quick-Fried Hot Diced Chicken, Sichuan Style

7 oz (200 g) chicken breasts and thighs
2 tbsp cornstarch (cornflour), dissolved in
   2 tbsp water
1/8 tsp salt, or to taste
2 tsp rice wine
1 1/2 tsp soy sauce
1 cup high stock (see p. 17)
1 tsp sesame oil

5 water chestnuts
1 hot red chili (chilli) pepper
1/2 cup (100 ml) vegetable oil
1 tsp ginger slices
2 tsp scallions, chopped
1 tsp garlic slices
1/8 tsp rice vinegar
1/8 tsp MSG

1. Skin, bone, and dice the chicken. Blend 1 tbsp of the cornstarch-water mixture with the salt and 1 tsp of the rice wine. Add the chicken and stir to coat well. Set aside.
2. In another bowl, mix the soy sauce, the remaining 1 tsp rice wine, the stock, the other 1 tbsp of cornstarch, MSG and the sesame oil into a sauce. Set aside. Peel and dice the water chestnuts. Seed the chili pepper and chop finely. Set aside.
3. Heat the oil in a wok over high heat to 225°F (110°C), or until small bubbles appear around the

edge of a piece of scallion green or ginger tossed into the oil. Add the chicken and chili pepper and stir-fry until the chicken turns red (see Illustration I).

4. Add the ginger, water chestnuts, scallions and garlic, and fry until fragrant. Stir in the sauce and sprinkle with the vinegar. Stir-fry about 30 seconds. Remove, and serve.

69. Braised Prawns, Chicken and Ham, Beijing Style

2 fresh prawns
9 oz (250 g) boneless chicken breast
1/2 oz (15 g) Chinese ham
1 tsp rice wine, or dry sherry
1 egg white
1/4 tsp salt, or to taste
1/2 oz (15 g) fresh or canned bamboo shoots

2 stalks of rape
2 tsp cornstarch (cornflour)
10 stalks of asparagus, fresh, canned or frozen
1/2 oz (15 g) dried bamboo shoot slices, soaked
4 cups (1 litre) chicken broth
2 tsp MSG

1. Shell, devein and remove the heads of the prawns. Mince the meat into a pulp and mix with the rice wine, egg white, MSG and salt. Slice the fresh or canned bamboo shoots and sprinkle each slice with dry cornstarch and spread with some of the prawn pulp.
2. Wash the rape leaves and shred. Chop 1 tsp of the ham very finely and garnish the prawns with the rape shreds and ham.
3. Place the prawns on a heat-proof dish and steam for 3 minutes. Remove and cut the prawn slices into rectangular pieces. Place in a wok. Cut asparagus into 1 inch (3cm) sections. Cut the chicken into thin slices and cut the 2 tsp ham into small diamonds. Cut cabbages into 1 inch sections. Cut the dried bamboo shoot slices into small floral patterns. Add all the meat and vegetables to the wok, along with the chicken stock. Bring to a boil, remove and serve.
Note: This is a popularized version of a recipe from the former imperial kitchen.

70. Scrambled Eggs with Tomatoes, Beijing Style

3 tomatoes
2 eggs
1 tsp salt, or to taste
4 tbsp vegetable oil

1/2 tsp scallions, shredded
1/2 tsp fresh ginger, shredded
1 1/2 tsp sugar
1/4 tsp MSG

1. Drop the tomatoes in boiling water for 30 seconds. Remove, drain, and peel. Cut in half, squeeze out the seeds, and chop coarsely.
2. Beat the eggs with the 1/4 tsp salt.
3. Heat 2 tbsp of the oil in a wok over high heat until the oil surface ripples. Pour in the eggs and cook , stirring constantly, until thickened. Remove from the wok and place in a dish. Add the other 2 tbsp of oil to the wok and reheat until very hot. Add the scallions and ginger and stir-fry for a few seconds. Then add the tomato, the remaining salt, sugar and MSG. Stir-fry about 30 seconds, then return the scrambled eggs to the wok. Stir to blend, remove, and serve.

71. Egg Dumplings, Chengdu-Sichuan Style

1 tsp dried shrimps
9 oz Chinese cabbage leaves
3 arrowheads
3 1/2 oz (100 g) minced pork
1/4 tsp scallions, chopped

1 tsp cornstarch, dissolved in 1 tsp water
4 1/2 tbsp vegetable oil
4 eggs
1/2 tsp salt, or to taste
5 oz high stock (see p. 17)

1. Soak the dried shrimps in hot water for 20 minutes. Remove, drain, and chop finely. Wash the Chinese cabbage leaves and cut into halves. Peel arrowheads and chop finely.
2. Mix minced pork with arrowheads, scallions, ginger, shrimps, cornstarch, and 1 tsp oil. Stir to blend well.
3. Beat the eggs. Add in 1/2 tsp of the salt.
4. Divide egg and pork into four portions respectively. Add 1 tbsp of the oil to a wok and heat over a low fire until barely hot. Pour in one portion of the egg and swirl it around to make a very thin pancake. Immediately add a portion of the pork mixture into the centre of the egg pancake. Fold up the pancake into a crescent dumpling with the pork filling inside. Remove. Add another tbsp of the oil and repeat until all the dumplings are made.
5. Pour the stock into a pot and the cabbage leaves. Bring to a boil and add 1/4 tsp salt. Add the dumplings. Simmer over low heat for 5 minutes and remove.

72. Stir-Fried Chicken Shreds with Jellyfish, Shandong-Liaoning Style

9 oz (250 g) edible dried jellyfish
1/4 tsp ginger, chopped
7 oz (200 g) chicken breast pieces
1 tbsp lightly beaten egg white
2 tbsp cornstarch (cornflour), dissolved in
    2 tbsp water

3 cups (750 ml) vegetable oil for deep-frying
1/4 tsp scallions, shredded
1 tsp rice wine
1/4 tsp salt, or taste
2 tsp sesame oil
1/2 tsp MSG

1. Soak the jellyfish in cold water for 3 hours. Wash and cut into 2 by 1 inch (5cm by 3cm) pieces. Plunge into boiling water, remove immediately, and drain. Set aside.
2. Skin the chicken and remove any tendons. Cut horizontally into slices about 1 inch (3cm) wide, then stack the slices and cut along the grain into shreds. Mix with the egg white and cornstarch and set aside.
3. Set the wok over high heat. Pour in the oil and heat to 150°F (70°C) warm, and add the chicken immediately. Stir gently until the chicken shreds separate, then remove rapidly. Drain well and set aside.
4. Pour the oil out of the wok, leaving only enough to cover the bottom. Heat the wok until the oil surface ripples. Add the scallions and stir. Add the jellyfish and chicken, then the rice wine, salt, MSG and ginger. Stir-fry about 30 seconds. Sprinkle with sesame oil, and serve.

73. White Fungus Peony Flowers, Beijing Style

3 1/2 oz (100 g) dried silver ears (white fungus,
    snow ears)
5 oz (150 g) chicken breast
3 oz (100 ml) vegetable oil
4 egg whites
1 whole egg
1 small tomato

9 fl oz (250 ml) clear stock (see p. 17)
5 tsp salt, or to taste
1 tbsp cornstarch (cornflour) dissolved in 1
    tbsp water
1/2 tsp chicken fat, melted
1 tsp MSG

1. Soak silver ears in warm water until soft. Wash well and remove the stems. Discard any discolored pieces.

2. Skin and bone the chicken breasts, mince into a pulp and mix with the 4 egg whites and 3 oz of the oil to make a paste.

3. Divide the silver ears into 20 equal portions. Spoon a bit of the chicken paste on each to resemble a white peony. Place on a heat-proof dish.

4. Beat the whole egg. Heat the remaining oil in a wok over medium heat. Pour in the egg and swirl the wok to make a thin pancake, cook until just dry (about 15 seconds), remove, and cut into shreds. Sprinkle on the chicken "cores" of the fungus "peonies". Place the dish of silver ears in a steamer and steam for 5 minutes. Remove and set aside.

5. Drop the tomato in boiling water for 30 seconds. Remove, drain and peel. Cut out the stem end, then make 3 vertical cuts, being careful to leave the tomato segments linked at the bottom. Spread the wedges apart to resemble a red peony, and place in the middle of the dish of fungus.

6. Pour the stock into a pot and add the salt and MSG. Bring to a boil. Stir in the cornstarch and add. Cook, stirring, until thickened slightly. Pour over the "peonies", sprinkle with chicken fat, and serve.

74. Stir-Fried Egg Floss, Kaifeng-Henan Style

7 egg yolks
3 egg whites
3/4 tsp salt, or to taste
1/8 tsp rice wine

2 cups (500 ml) vegetable oil; uses about 1/2
    cup or 125 ml
1/8 tsp MSG

1. Beat the egg yolks and whites in a bowl and stir in the salt, rice wine, and MSG.
2. Heat the oil in a wok over low heat, to very hot about 350°F (180°C), or until smoke rises. Pour the eggs through a perforated spoon into the oil and deep-fry until yellow. The egg will cook into threads as thin as hair. Remove the egg threads from the oil and drain well. Loosen the egg threads into a light, airy floss, place in a dish, and serve.

75. Egg Pancakes, Beijing Style

3 eggs   1 tsp salt, or to taste
1/2 tsp scallions, chopped   5 tsp vegetable oil

1. Beat the eggs in a bowl and add the scallions and salt, mixing well.
2. Heat the oil in a wok over high heat until the surface ripples. Add the eggs and swirl the pan so
the eggs cover the surface evenly. Turn the heat to low and cook until the bottom of the pancake is
set and browned, turn and cook until browned on the other side. Remove and serve.

76. Steamed Egg Custard, Beijing Style

3 eggs
2 tsp soy sauce
1/4 tsp salt, or to taste
1 tsp sesame oil

1 1/2 cups (350 ml) warm or cold water
1 tbsp dried shrimps
1/2 tsp scallions, shredded

1. Soak the dried shrimps in warm water until soft. Drain and chop finely.
2. Whisk together the eggs, soy sauce, salt, and sesame oil in a heat-proof bowl. Blend in the water.
3. Place the bowl in a steamer and steam for 15 minutes. Remove, sprinkle with the shrimps and scallions, and serve.

77. Duck Rolls, Beijing Style

skin from 1 1/2 ducks, cooked
7 oz (200 g) duck thigh meat
3 eggs
1/2 tsp soy sauce
1/4 tsp rice wine
1/4 tsp salt, or to taste
1/4 tsp ground Sichuan peppercorn
1/4 tsp ginger, chopped

1/4 tsp scallions, chopped
1/4 tsp water chestnut, chopped
1/2 tsp sesame oil
4 tbsp (50 g) cornstarch (cornflour)
1 cup (100 g) dried bread crumbs
3 cups (750 ml) duck fat or vegetable oil,
    or a combination, for deep-frying
1/2 tsp MSG

1. Cut the duck skin into 2 by 2 1/2 inch (6cm X 5cm) pieces.
2. Mince the duck meat. Stir in the soy sauce, rice wine, salt, MSG, pepper, ginger, scallions, water chestnut, and sesame oil, and mix well. Divide duck mixture to portions, one portion for one piece of the duck skins. Place one portion of the duck mixture at one end of each piece of the skin and roll into cylinders about 3/4 inch (16.5 mm) in diameter.
3. Beat the eggs. Roll the cylinders in the cornstarch, then dip them in the egg and coat well with the bread crumbs.
4. Heat the oil or duck fat, or both, in a wok over high heat to moderately hot, about 375°F (190°C). Remove the wok from the fire, or turn off the heat, and carefully add the duck rolls. Stir a few times and return the wok to the heat or turn the heat back on. Deep-fry the rolls until they float to the surface. Turn the heat to low and deep-fry for 2 to 3 more minutes, or until all the rolls begin turning brown. Turn the heat to high and deep-fry for 30 more seconds. Remove, drain well, and serve.

FISH AND
SEAFOOD DISHES

78. Deep-Fried Yellow Croaker with Sweet-and-Sour Sauce, Shanghai Style

1 whole yellow croaker about 1 1/2 lb (750
   g) (or similar fish)
1/2 tsp salt
6 cups (1,500 ml) vegetable oil for deep-frying;
   uses about 7 oz (200 ml)
1/2 tsp scallions, chopped
1/4 tsp fresh ginger, chopped

1/2 tsp garlic, chopped
3 1/2 oz (100 ml) vinegar
2 tsp soy sauce
10 oz (300 ml) clear stock (see p. 17)
14 tbsp (200 g) sugar
10 tbsp (150 g) cornstarch (cornflour), dissolved in 5 tbsp water

1. Draw, scale, and wash the fish. Blot dry. Make 5 to 7 diagonal slashes about 1/4 inch deep at even intervals on each side. Rub salt in the slashes and dust all over with flour.
2. Heat the oil in a wok to about 350°F (180°C). Hold the fish by the tail and carefully lower it into the oil. Slide a wok scoop or spatula under the fish to keep it from sticking to the wok and deep-fry until the slashes open, about 2 minutes. Carefully turn the fish upside down, holding it against the side of the wok, and deep-fry another 2 minutes. Continue to turn the fish and deep-fry it until the skin is brown on all sides. Finish by laying the fish flat in the oil and pressing the head down with the scoop until it browns. Remove, drain and place on a large oval serving dish.
3. Pour all but 7 tbsp of the oil out of the wok. Heat until the oil surface ripples. Add the scallions, ginger, garlic, vinegar, and soy sauce. Add the stock, sugar, and cornstarch. Cook, stirring, until the sauce thickens. Pour over the fish and serve.

79. Deep-Fried Mandarin Fish, Beijing Style

1 whole mandarin fish, about 3 1/2 lb (1,500 g) or other whole freshwater fish such as perch, bass
2 tsp scallions, chopped
2 tsp ginger, sliced
1 tsp rice wine
5 tsp salt, or to taste
1/8 tsp pepper
1/4 tsp sesame oil
2 tbsp cornstarch (cornflour) dissolved in 2 tbsp water
8 tbsp dry cornstarch
4 tbsp ketchup

4 tsp Worcestershire sauce
7 tsp sugar
5 fl oz (150 ml) chicken stock
4 cups (1 litre) vegetable oil for deep-frying; uses about 5 oz (150 ml)
1 tbsp garlic, chopped
1 oz (25 g) pineapple, diced
1 oz (25 g) green beans or pea pods, diced
1 oz (25 g) carrot, diced
4 cups (1,000 ml) vegetable oil, consumes about 5 fl oz or 150 ml
1 tsp MSG

1. Prepare and wash the fish. Chop off the head and tail. Cut the fish in half along the spine and remove the spine and rib bones. Make criss-cross scores on the flesh side and cut into 1 1/2 inch (4cm) square pieces.
2. Mix together the scallions, ginger, rice wine, 1/2 tsp MSG, 4 3/4 tsp of the salt, the pepper, and the sesame oil, and rub on the sides of the fish. Dip the fish pieces, head, and tail into the dissolved cornstarch and dust with the dry cornstarch.
3. Mix the ketchup, Worcestershire sauce, 1/4 tsp of the salt, 1/2 tsp of the MSG, the sugar, sesame oil, chicken stock and 1 tsp of the dissolved cornflour into a sauce. Set aside.
4. Heat the oil in a wok to about 350°F (180°C). Deep-fry the fish head and tail for 2 minutes. Remove and place on the narrow sides of an oval fish dish. Add the fish pieces to the oil and deep-fry for 2 minutes, or until cooked. Remove, drain, and place in the dish.
5. Heat 4 tbsp oil in another wok until the oil surface ripples. Add the garlic and 1 tbsp scallions and stir-fry until fragrant. Add the pineapple, green beans or pea pods, and carrot. Add the sauce and bring to a boil. Stir in 7 tbsp of the hot oil used for deep-frying. When the sauce bubbles, pour it over the fish, and serve.

80. Dry-Fried Yellow Croaker, Northeast China Style

1 whole yellow croaker about 2 lb (1 kg)
  (or similar fish)
2 tsp rice wine
1 tsp soy sauce
1 egg

2 tsp salt, or to taste
4 tsp cornstarch (cornflour)
6 cups (1,500 ml) vegetable oil for deep-frying
2 tsp spiced pepper-salt (see p. 10)
2 tsp Worcestershire sauce

1. Draw, scale and wash the fish. Make 3.5 cm diagonal slashes on each side. Rub the rice wine and soy sauce on the sides and let marinate about 15 minutes.
2. Mix the egg, salt, and cornflour into a paste and coat the fish.
3. Heat the oil in a wok to 350°F (180°C) . Deep-fry the fish until the coating hardens. Remove and drain. Reheat the oil to 400°F (205°C), and deep-fry the fish until brown. Remove, drain well, place on a dish. Serve with two small dishes of spiced pepper-salt and Worcestershire sauce.

81. Braised Hairtail in Soy Sauce, Beijing Style

1 lb (500 g) hairtail (or similar fish)
9 oz (300 ml) vegetable oil for deep-frying
2 cups (500 ml) high stock (see p. 17)
5 tsp soy sauce
1 tsp salt, or to taste
1 tsp scallions, chopped

1 tbsp sugar
1 tsp fresh ginger, sliced
1 clove star anise
1 tbsp cornstarch (cornflour) dissolved in
  1 tbsp water
1 tsp hot red chili (chilli) oil

1. Clean and wash the fish. Cut off the head and fins and chop crosswise into 4 inch (10 cm) sections.
2. Heat the oil in a wok over high heat to about 350°F (175°C), or until a piece of scallion green or ginger sizzles and moves around quickly when dropped into the oil. Add the fish sections and deep-fry until brown. Remove and drain. Pour the oil out of the wok, leaving enough to cover the bottom, about 2 tbsp. Add the fish, rice wine, stock, sugar, soy sauce, salt, scallions, ginger, and star anise. Cover, bring to a boil and simmer over low heat for 10 minutes. Remove the fish and place in a dish.
3. Add the cornstarch-water mixture to the wok and cook, stirring, until thickened. Sprinkle 1 tsp hot red chili oil over the sauce, pour over the fish, and serve.

82. Dry-Fried Hairtail, Beijing Style

2 fresh hairtails
4 tsp salt
2 tsp rice wine
5 1/2 tbsp flour

5 fl oz (150 ml) vegetable oil
1/2 tsp spiced pepper-salt
1/4 tsp Worcestershire sauce

1. Draw and clean fish. Chop off head and tails. Make criss-cross scores on both sides of fish. Chop fish crosswise into 1 1/2 inch (4cm) sections. Marinated fish with salt and rice wine.
2. Heat oil in a wok to very hot, about 350°F (180°C). Dust fish pieces with flour and add to the oil. Deep-fried until brown. Remove and drain, place fish in a dish. Serve with spiced pepper-salt and Worcestershire sauce as the dips.

83. Fragrant Creamed Hairtail, Shanghai Style

5 oz (150 g) hairtail, scaled and boned (or fish fillets)
1/2 tsp rice wine
1 tsp salt, or to taste
1/4 tsp pepper
1/2 tsp sesame oil

5 tbsp cornstarch (cornflour)
2 cups (500 ml) vegetable oil for deep-frying
4 oz (120 ml) milk
1 tbsp ketchup
1 1/2 tsp ground roasted sesame seeds

1. Cut the fish into 2 inch by 3/4 inch (5 cm by 2 cm) pieces. Mix the rice wine, 1/4 tsp of the salt, the pepper, and the sesame oil and add to the fish. Let marinate.

2. Dust the fish pieces with 4 tbsp cornflour. Dissolve the remaining 1 tbsp of the cornflour in 2 tsp water. Set aside.

3. Heat the oil in a wok over high heat to very hot, about 350°F (180°C). Add the fish piece by piece and deep-fry until brown. Remove, drain, and place in a dish. Pour all but 1 tbsp of the oil out of the wok. Add 4 tbsp water and bring to a boil over high heat. Add the milk and ketchup, and stir until the mixture boils again. Add the remaining 3/4 tsp salt (or to taste), the cornstarch-water mixture. Cook, stirring, until thickened. Pour the sauce over the fish, sprinkle with ground sesame seed, and serve.

84. Five-Coloured Fish Shreds, Beijing Style

1 lb (500 g) fresh fish filets, skinned
3 1/2 oz (100 g) dried Chinese black mushrooms, soaked in hot water until soft and
then shredded
5 oz (150 g) carrot, shredded
1/2 tsp salt, or to taste
2 tsp rice wine
1/4 tsp pepper
2 egg whites
3 tbsp dry cornstarch (cornflour)

1 tsp cornstarch dissolved in 1 tsp water
1/2 tsp sesame oil
5 tsp chicken stock
1/2 tsp sugar
2 cups (500 ml) vegetable oil for deep-frying
3 1/2 oz (100 g) green pepper, shredded
3 1/2 oz (100 g) bean sprouts
1 tsp scallions, chopped
1 tsp fresh ginger, chopped
1 tsp MSG

1. Cut the fish into 2 inch (5 cm) sections, then into slices and 3/4 inch (2 cm) shreds.
2. Mix 1/4 tsp of the salt, the rice wine, 1/8 tsp of the pepper, the egg whites, and the cornstarch into a batter. Stir in 2 tbsp of the sesame oil and rub the fish pieces with the batter. Set aside.
3. Blanch the mushrooms and carrots briefly in boiling water. Rinse in cold water and drain immediately.
4. Mix together the remaining 1/4 tsp of the salt and the 1/2 tsp of MSG, the chicken stock, the remaining 1/4 tsp of the sesame oil, and remaining 1/8 tsp of the pepper, the sugar and the cornstarch-water mixture into a sauce.
5. Heat the oil to moderately hot about 230°F (110°C). Add the mushrooms, carrot, green pepper, bean sprouts, scallions and ginger. Stir-fry 1 minute. Add the fish and rice wine and stir. Pour in the sauce and stir-fry to blend all the ingredients together. Remove and serve.

85. Stir-Fried Fish Cubes, Shandong Style

10 1/2 oz (300 g) fish filets
1 egg white
1 tbsp cornstarch (cornflour) dissolved in 1 tbsp water
2 oz (50 g) bamboo shoots (or canned)
3 1/2 oz (100 ml) high stock (see p. 17)
10 peas
1/4 tsp rice wine

1 tsp salt, or to taste
1 tbsp soy sauce
1 1/2 tbsp scallions, cut diagonally in 1/2 inch (1 cm) sections
2 cloves garlic, sliced
4 cups (1,000 ml) vegetable oil for deep-frying
1 tsp MSG

1. Cut the fish into 1/2 inch (1 cm) dice. Mix the egg white with 2 tsp of the dissolved cornstarch and coat the fish. Cut the bamboo shoots into 1/2 inch (1 cm) cubes.
2. Mix together the stock, peas, MSG, salt, the other 1 tsp of the dissolved cornflour, and the rice wine. Set aside.
3. Heat the oil in a wok to about 250°F (120°C), or until small bubbles sizzle around a piece of scallion green or ginger tossed into the oil. Add the fish dice, stirring to keep them separate, and remove immediately.
4. Pour all but 2 tbsp of oil out of the wok. Heat over high heat to very hot, or until the oil surface ripples and a haze appears on the surface of the oil. Add the scallions and garlic, and stir-fry until fragrant. Add the bamboo shoots and stir in the sauce. Add the fish. Stir-fry a few more seconds, remove, and serve.

86. Quick-Boiled Fish Slices, Hangzhou Style

9 oz (250 g) fish filet, skinned and boned.
1 tsp salt, or to taste
1/2 tsp rice wine
2 cups (500 ml) fish stock

1 oz (25 g) bamboo shoots, sliced
a few green leaves, washed and cut into halves
1 tsp melted lard or vegetable oil
1/4 tsp MSG

1. Wash the fish and cut into 1/4 inch by 1 inch (3 cm by 2 cm) slices. Add 1/2 tsp of the salt and the rice wine and let marinate.
2. Heat a pot of water to a boil. Add the fish and remove immediately. Drain and place in a bowl. Pour the stock into a wok and heat to boiling. Skim off any foam and add the remaining 1/2 tsp salt, the MSG, bamboo shoots and leaves. Return the stock to a boil and pour over the fish. Sprinkle with the lard or oil, and serve.

87. Tender-Fried Fish Slices, Hangzhou Style

3 1/2 oz (100 g) fish filet, skinned and boned
1 egg white
2 tsp cornstarch
1/2 tsp rice wine

1/2 tsp salt
1/2 tsp scallion sections
1/2 tsp garlic mash
4 tbsp vegetable oil

1. Wash the fish and dry well and cut into slices. Mix the egg white, cornstarch, and salt into a batter. Coat the fish slices with the batter.
2. Heat the oil to very hot. Add the fish and stir-fry until cooked. Remove and drain.
3. Reheat the wok, add scallions and garlic and fry until fragrant. Add the fish and sprinkle with the rice wine. Add the rest of the batter. Tip the wok to swirl the mass. Turn mass over and remove.

88. Fish with Hot Sauce, Beijing Style

1 whole fish, (yellow croaker, carp, mullet or bass) about 2 1/2 lb (1,000 g), cleaned and scaled
1 tsp salt, or to taste
1 cup (500 ml) oil for deep-frying
1 tsp scallions, shredded
1 tsp fresh ginger, chopped
2 hot red chili (chilli) peppers, seeded and shredded

1 tsp green pepper, shredded
3 1/2 oz (100 g) onions, shredded
4 tsp soy sauce
1 tsp rice wine
2 tsp sugar
1 tsp cornstarch (cornflour) dissolved in 1 tsp water
1/4 tsp MSG

1. Wash and dry the fish. Make 3 to 5 diagonal slashes on each side and rub the skin and slashes with the salt.

2. Heat the oil in a wok over high heat to very hot about 350°F (175°C) or until a piece of scallion green or ginger sizzles and moves around quickly when tossed in the oil. Add the scallions and onions and ginger and the fish and deep-fry until both sides are brown. Remove, drain and place on a serving dish.

3. Pour all but 2 to 3 tbsp of the oil out of the wok, leaving only enough to cover the bottom. Heat until the oil surface ripples. Add the hot red chili, green pepper, and onion shreds, and stir-fry until fragrant. Stir in the soy sauce, rice wine, sugar, MSG, and ginger. Add 1 cup water and bring to a boil. Stir the cornstarch-water mixture and add to the wok. Cook, stirring, until the sauce thickens. Remove, pour over the fish, and serve.

89. Braised Fish with Garlic, Sichuan Style

1 whole fish, about 1 1/2 lb (750 g), head and tail removed (carp, perch, sea bass, mullet)
1/2 tsp salt, or to taste
4 cups (1 litre) vegetable oil for deep-frying; uses about 5 oz (150 ml)
3 1/2 oz (100 g) garlic
1 hot red chili (chilli) pepper, stem removed and chopped
1 tsp ginger, chopped

1 1/2 cup (400 ml) fish or meat stock
1 tbsp sugar
3 1/2 tsp soy sauce
2 1/2 tbsp rice wine
2 tsp vinegar
1 tbsp scallions, chopped in sections
1 tsp cornstarch (cornflour) dissolved in 1 tsp water
5 tsp sesame oil
1/4 tsp MSG

1. Cut the fish into slices about 1 1/2 inch (4 cm) long. Rub with the salt and let marinate for 15 minutes.
2. Heat the oil in a wok to about 350°F (175°C), or until a piece of scallion green or ginger sizzles and moves around quickly when tossed into the oil. Add the garlic and deep-fry until fragrant. Remove and drain. Add the fish pieces and deep-fry until browned. Remove, drain well and set aside.
3. Pour all but 7 tbsp of the oil out of the wok. Add the garlic, red chili pepper, and ginger. Stir-fry until fragrant. Add the fish, stock, sugar, soy sauce, and rice wine, and simmer over low heat for 15 minutes. Remove the fish and place in a serving dish. Add the vinegar, scallions, MSG, and cornstarch mixture to the wok. Raise the heat and cook, stirring, until the sauce thickens. Add the sesame oil, pour the sauce over the fish, and serve.

90. Steamed Carp, Suzhou Style

1 whole fresh carp about 1 lb (500 g) (or trout and other firm-fleshed fresh-water fish)
5 tsp rice wine
1 tsp salt, or to taste
4 black mushrooms, sliced and soaked

4 bamboo shoots, sliced
2 tbsp lean pork, diced and marinated in sugar
4 slices Chinese ham, steamed
2 1/2 tbsp lard or vegetable oil
2 tsp scallions, chopped in 1-inch sections
1 tsp ginger, sliced

1. Wash the fish and make 2 to 3 X-shaped slashes on each side. Rub with the rice wine and let marinate. Place on a heat-proof dish and sprinkle with the salt, mushrooms, bamboo shoots, and diced pork. Place the ham, lard, scallions, and ginger on top.
2. Place the dish in a steamer and steam for 10 to 15 minutes, or until the fish is cooked through. Discard the scallions and ginger, and serve.

91. Steamed Carp in Egg Custard, Beijing-Hebei Style

1 whole carp, about 3/4 lb (350 g), with head and tail (substitute trout or other firm-flesh freshwater fish)
4 eggs
1/2 tsp salt, or to taste
1 tbsp rice wine

1 oz (30 ml) clear stock (see p. 17)
1 tsp soy sauce
2 tsp sesame oil
1/2 tsp scallions, chopped
1/2 tsp ginger, chopped
1 tsp MSG

1. Clean and wash the fish. Blanch in boiling water and drain.
2. Beat the eggs in a heat-proof bowl and stir in the salt, rice wine, MSG, 4 tsp of the stock and mix well. Place fish in the bowl with the egg mixture. Place the bowl in a steamer and steam for 10 to 15 minutes, or until the custard is set.
3. Mix the soy sauce, sesame oil, the remaining 2 tsp of the stock, the scallions, and the ginger into a sauce. Pour over the fish and serve.

92. Braised Prawns, Shanghai Style

7 prawns, whole
3 1/2 oz (100 ml) vegetable oil or lard
1/2 tsp scallions, chopped
1/2 tsp fresh ginger, chopped
4 tsp rice wine
1 tsp salt, or to taste
1 tsp sugar

3 1/2 oz (100 ml) stock
1 1/2 tbsp tomato sauce
1/4 tsp soy sauce
1 tbsp cornstarch (cornflour) dissolved in
    1 tbsp water
3 1/2 fl oz vegetable oil

1. Wash the prawns well. Twist off the heads and feet but do not shell, cut the shells along the back and devein with a tooth pick, or small knife. Rinse again under cold water.
2. Heat 6 tbsp oil or lard in a wok until the oil surface ripples. Add the scallions and ginger. Add the prawns and stir-fry about 30 seconds. Add the rice wine, cover the wok, and cook for 30 seconds. Add the salt, sugar and stock. Bring to a boil over high heat, cover, and simmer over low heat for 3 minutes. Add the tomato sauce and soy sauce and turn the heat to high. Boil until the sauce is reduced. Stir in the cornstarch mixture and cook, stirring, until thickened. Add 1 tbsp oil or lard and stir-fry to blend. Remove and serve.

93. Prawn Goldfish, Beijing-North China Style

6 prawns, in shells
1 tsp salt, or to taste
1 1/2 tsp rice wine
2 1/2 oz (75 g) boneless chicken breast
1/2 egg whites
2 tsp (10 ml) vegetable oil
2 tbsp flour
6 red cherries, pitted and halved

1 silver ear (white fungus), soaked in luke-warm water until soft
3 1/2 oz (100 ml) chicken and duck or chicken stock
2 tsp cornstarch (cornflour) dissolved in 2 tsp water
1 tbsp melted chicken fat
3/4 tsp MSG

1. Remove the heads from the prawns and shell, but do not remove the tails. Devein and rinse. Score prawns along the vein line, but do not cut through. Flaten prawns from the openings. Make cross scores lightly on the prawns. Mix the prawns with 1/2 tsp of the salt, 1 tsp of the rice wine, ginger, and the MSG, and let marinate for 10 minutes.

2. Mince the chicken into a pulp and add the egg whites, 1/8 tsp of the salt, and 2 tsp oil. Stir vigorously in one direction for 1 minute, or until the mixture stiffens.

3. Dust the tops of the prawns with flour and spread with the chicken mixture, molding it in the shape of a goldfish body. Place 2 cherry halves on each as eyes and a small piece of silver ear on the back of each as a fin. Place "goldfish" on a heat-proof dish and steam for 10 minutes. Set aside.

4. Bring the stock to a boil. Add the remaining 1/4 tsp MSG, 1/2 tsp of salt, and 1/2 tsp of the rice wine. Skim off any foam and add the cornstarch mixture. Cook, stirring, until thickened. Pour the sauce over the goldfish, sprinkle with the melted chicken fat, and serve.

94. Oil-Braised Prawns, Beijing Style

5 prawns, in shells, with heads
2 fl oz (50 ml) vegetable oil
1 tbsp fresh ginger, shredded
1/2 cup (120 ml) high stock (see p. 17)
1 tbsp sugar

1 tbsp rice wine
1/4 tsp salt, or to taste
1/4 tsp sesame oil
1 tbsp scallions, shredded
1/4 tsp MSG

1. Remove the heads from the prawns and set aside. Remove the legs, shell, devein and wash. Cut each prawn body into 3 equal sections.

2. Heat the oil in a wok until moderately hot. Add the prawn heads and ginger. Use a scoop to press the heads against the sides of the wok so the fat seeps out, colouring the oil red. Add the prawn sections and stir-fry for 1 minute. Add the stock, sugar, rice wine, MSG, and salt. Simmer over low heat for 5 to 6 minutes, or until the prawns are just cooked.

3. Remove the prawn heads and place in a dish with the prawn sections on top. Boil the sauce in the wok over high heat until thickened. Sprinkle with sesame oil. Add the scallions and garlic shreds, pour the sauce over the prawns, and serve.

95. Drunken Fresh Shrimps, Sichuan Style

10 1/2 oz (300 g) live fresh-water shrimps
3 1/2 oz (100 g) scallion white
1 oz (25 g) scallions, chopped
15 Sichuan roasted peppercorns
1/4 tsp salt, or to taste

2 tsp soy sauce
2 tsp sesame oil
1 tbsp meat stock
2 tsp strong white liquor
1/4 tsp MSG

1. Crush the peppercorns and the scallion white together, and mix with salt, soy sauce, sesame oil, stock, MSG to make a dipping sauce.
2. Wash the shrimps well to rid them of any sand. Cut off the whiskers and feet, wash again, and drain. Place in a bowl and set aside.
3. A few minutes before serving, pour the liquor over the shrimps, add chopped scallions and cover the bowl with a dish. Invert the bowl and weight it so the shrimps cannot get out.
4. To eat, dip the live shrimps in the dipping sauce.

96. Deep-Fried Fresh Shrimps, Tianjin Style

1 lb (500 g) fresh or frozen shrimps
3 1/2 oz (100 g) flour

2 tsp salt, or to taste
2 cups (500 ml) vegetable oil for deep-frying

1. Shell and devein the shrimps and wash well. Drain and sprinkle with the salt. Let marinate for 15 minutes. Mix the shrimps with the flour until well coated.
2. Heat the oil in a wok to about 350°F (175°C), or until a piece of scallion green or ginger sizzles and moves about when dropped into the oil. Add the shrimps and deep-fry until browned. Remove, drain well, and serve.

97. Tender-Fried Prawn Slices, Beijing Style

5 oz (150 g) prawns, without heads
2 1/2 tsp rice wine
1/2 tsp salt, or to taste
1 egg white
2 tsp cornstarch (cornflour) dissolved in 1 tbsp water
1 oz (25 g) bamboo shoots, sliced

2 tsp soy sauce
1 tsp scallions, shredded
1/2 tsp garlic shoots, in 1/2 inch (1 cm) sections
1 tsp fresh ginger, chopped
2 cups (1/2 litre) vegetable oil for deep-frying
1/2 tsp sesame oil
1/2 tsp MSG

1. Shell and devein the prawns. Wash and drain. Cut diagonally into 1/4 inch slices.
2. Mix together 1/4 tsp of the MSG, 1 1/2 tsp of the rice wine, the salt, egg white, and all but 1 tsp of the cornstarch. Add the prawns and coat well. Let marinate.
3. Drop the bamboo shoot slices into boiling water to cover for about 30 seconds. Drain well and cut into 1/4 inch slices, set aside.
4. Make a sauce by mixing together the soy sauce, the remaining rice wine, the shredded scallions, the garlic shoots, the ginger, the bamboo shoots, and the remaining cornstarch with 1 tsp water.
5. Heat the oil in a wok over high heat to 350°F (170°C), or until a piece of scallion green or ginger sizzles noisily and moves around quickly when tossed into the oil. Add the prawn slices, stir with chopsticks, and immediately remove from the oil. Drain well.
6. Pour the oil out of the wok, leaving only enough to cover the bottom. Add the prawn slices. Stir the sauce and add. Cook, stirring, until thickened. Sprinkle with sesame oil. Remove and serve.

98. Braised Turtle in Soy Sauce, Sichuan Style

1 live soft-shelled turtle about 2 lb (1 kg)
9 oz (250 g) boneless pork
8 chicken wings
5 tbsp lard or vegetable oil
4 oz (100 g) garlic, sliced
2 tbsp ginger, sliced
3 tbsp (50 g) scallions, chopped, white parts only
3 1/2 tbsp soy sauce

1 1/2 tbsp brown sugar
1 tsp salt, or to taste
2 tbsp rice wine
4 1/4 cups (1 litre) chicken stock
2 1/2 cups (650 ml) meat stock
1/4 tsp pepper
1 tbsp sesame oil
1/4 tsp MSG

1. Chop off the turtle's head and drain off the blood. Scrape off the hard outer skin, remove the hard shell, and gut. Wash thoroughly and chop off the feet. Cut the turtle into 3 inch (7 cm) chunks.
2. Chop the pork into 2 oz (50 g) pieces. Cut off the tips of the chicken wings and chop each into 2 pieces. Parboil the pork and chicken wings in boiling water for 1 minute. Remove. Place garlic in a heat-proof bowl and steam until tender.
3. Heat the oil or lard in a wok over medium heat until warm, about 210°F (100°C). Add half the ginger and scallions and stir-fry until fragrant. Add the pork and chicken wings and stir-fry for 5 minutes. Add the soy sauce, brown sugar, salt, 1 tbsp of the rice wine, and the chicken stock. Bring to a boil and simmer over a low fire until the sauce thickens.
4. Pour the meat stock into another wok and heat. When it comes to a boil add the rest of the ginger and scallions, and the rest of the rice wine. Add the turtle pieces to boil for 2 minutes. Remove. Add turtle pieces to the pork and chicken wings, simmer for 10 minutes over low heat. Add the pepper and continue simmering until the turtle meat is very tender. Remove the garlic to the stock. When the sauce thickened, pick up the pork in the wok (the pork can be used for other dish). Remove the chicken wings to the bottom of a dish. Stir in MSG and sesame oil in stock. Place the turtle on top with the sauce.

99. Stewed Turtle, Shandong Style

1 live soft-shelled turtle, about 2 lb (1 kg)
1 lb (500 g) boned chicken
3 1/2 oz (100 ml) vegetable oil or lard
1/2 tsp scallions, chopped
1/2 tsp fresh ginger, chopped

1/2 tsp garlic, chopped
5 whole Sichuan peppercorns
3 1/2 tbsp soy sauce
4 cups (1 litre) clear stock (see p. 17)
2 tsp rice wine

1. Cut off the turtle's head and drain off all the blood. Place in a pot of cold water to cover and bring to a boil. Remove the turtle and scrape off the black skin. Remove the hard upper shell and gut. Chop off the claws. Wash the turtle well and chop into 3/4 inch (2 cm) squares. Chop the chicken into 3/4 inch (2 cm) pieces and blanch briefly in boiling water for 2 minutes.

2. Heat oil or lard in a wok over high heat to about 350°F (175° C), or until a piece of scallion green or ginger sizzles and moves around quickly when dropped into the oil. Add the scallions, ginger, garlic, and peppercorns, and stir-fry until fragrant. Add the turtle, chicken, and soy sauce, and stir-fry for 3 minutes. Add the stock, and simmer over low heat for 1 1/2 hours. Then turn the heat to high and bring to a full boil. Skim off the foam and add the rice wine. Remove and serve.

Note: This dish features tender and succulent meat in a subtly-flavoured clear soup.

100. Stir-Fried Eels, Chongqing-Sichuan Style

1 lb (500 g) live eel
6 tsp fermented soybeans
3 1/2 oz (100 g) celery or garlic shoots,
chopped into 1 inch (3 cm)
3 1/2 oz (100 ml) vegetable oil
5 tsp rice wine
5 tsp soy sauce

1 1/2 tsp sugar
1/2 tsp fresh ginger, sliced
1/2 tsp garlic, sliced
1 scallions, chopped into 1 inch (3 cm) sections
1 tsp vinegar
1/4 tsp ground Sichuan peppercorns

1. Cut off the head and tail of the eel. Slit open the belly and remove the entrails. Cut off the meat along the backbone and discard the bone. Cut the meat into 2 inch (5 cm) slices.
2. Heat the oil in a wok to 400°F (205°C), or until a piece of scallion green or ginger browns quickly when tossed into the oil and a haze appears above the surface. Add the eel and stir-fry until barely cooked. Stir in the soybean, celery or garlic shoots, rice wine, soy sauce, sugar, ginger, garlic, and scallions. Stir-fry for about 30 seconds. Sprinkle with a little cold water and continue stir-frying until the sauce is almost completely reduced. Sprinkle with vinegar. Remove, sprinkle with the ground peppercorns, and serve.

101. Sea Cucumbers with Carrot, Northeast China Style

1 lb (500 g) fresh or reconstituted sea cucumbers
1 carrot
5 fl oz (500 ml) melted lard or vegetable oil
1/2 tsp scallions, shredded
1/2 tsp ginger, shredded
1/4 tsp garlic, sliced
1 tsp rice wine

1 tbsp soy sauce
4 fl oz (120 ml) high stock (see p. 17)
1/2 tsp sugar
1 tsp salt, or to taste
1 tbsp cornstarch (cornflour) dissolved in 2 tsp water
1/4 tsp sesame oil
1/4 tsp MSG

1. Cut the sea cucumbers open at the stomach and clean. Wash well and slice. Blanch in boiling water for 1 minute, remove, and drain. Slice the carrot thinly.
2. Heat the oil in a wok to about 350°F (170°C), or until a piece of scallion green or ginger sizzles and moves around when tossed into the oil. Add the sea cucumber and deep-fry for 30 seconds. Remove, drain, and set aside.
3. Pour all but a thin film of oil out of the wok. Heat the oil, add the scallions, ginger and garlic. Add the carrot slices. Stir, then, add the rice wine, soy sauce, stock, sea cucumber, sugar, MSG, and salt. When the stock comes to a boil, add the cornstarch mixture and cook, stirring, until thickened. Sprinkle with the sesame oil. Remove and serve.

102. Sea Cucumbers and Pigeon Eggs, Beijing Style·

1 1/2 lb (750 g) fresh or reconstituted sea
  cucumbers
15 pigeon eggs
15 Chinese cabbage hearts
2 tsp salt, or to taste
1 tsp soy sauce
5 tsp rice wine

1/2 tsp scallions, chopped
1/2 tsp fresh ginger, chopped
7 oz (200 ml) chicken stock
1 tbsp melted chicken fat
3 1/2 fl oz (100 ml) vegetable oil for deep-frying
1 tsp MSG

1. Cut the sea cucumbers at the stomach, and gut. Leave whole. Hard-boil the pigeon eggs, let cool, and shell. Halve the cabbage hearts lengthwise and chop into 2 1/2 inch (7cm) sections.
2. Rub the sea cucumbers with 1 tsp of the salt. Plunge into boiling water for 2 minutes, remove and drain. Blanch the cabbage hearts briefly in the salted boiling water, remove, drain and set aside.
3. Put the sea cucumbers in a wok and add the soy sauce, the remaining 1 tsp salt, the rice wine, sugar, scallions, ginger, chicken stock, and MSG. Bring to a boil and simmer for 2 minutes. Add the cornstarch-water mixture and cook, stirring, until thickened. Arrange the sea cucumbers and cabbage hearts alternately in a circle on a plate, and sprinkle with the melted chicken fat.
4. Heat the oil in a wok until the oil surface ripples. Add the eggs and deep-fry until golden. Arrange the eggs around the sea cucumbers and serve.

103. Scallops with Steamed Egg White, Shandong-Liaoning Style

3 1/2 oz (100 g) dried scallops
10 egg whites
2 tsp rice wine
2 tsp ginger, chopped finely
1/4 tsp salt, or to taste
2 tbsp cornstarch (cornflour) dissolved in 2

tbsp water
9 fl oz (250 ml) chicken and duck or chicken stock
2 tsp melted chicken fat
1/2 tsp MSG

1. Rinse the dried scallops and rub off any white film on their surface. Wash and place in a heat-proof bowl, with 9 oz (250 ml) water. Steam in a steamer for 1 1/2 hours, replenishing water as needed. Drain, reserving the stock. Let the scallops stand until cool enough to handle, then shred by hand, discarding the hard muscles. Return the scallop shreds to the water to marinate.
2. Whisk together the egg whites, 5 1/2 oz (150 ml) of the stock, 1 tsp of the rice wine, 1 tsp of the ginger, and 1/8 tsp of the salt. Mix well, remove the scum on the surface. Place in a heat-proof bowl and steam over low heat for about 10 minutes. Pour into a serving bowl.
3. Heat the remaining stock in a wok or pot. Add the scallops, the MSG, the remaining 1 tsp rice wine, the remaining 1 tsp ginger, and the remaining 1/8 tsp salt. Bring to a boil and skim off any foam. Add the cornstarch-water mixture and cook, stirring, until thickened. Sprinkle with the melted chicken fat, pour over the egg whites, and serve.

104. Beijing Hot Pot, Beijing Style

1 lb (500 g) fresh or reconstituted sea cucumbers

3 prawns

5 oz (150 g) bamboo shoots (or canned bamboo shoots)

1 lb (500 g) cellophane noodles; cut into 6 inch (15 cm) sections

9 oz (250 g) boneless chicken, cooked

3 1/2 oz (100 g) small fresh or canned mushrooms

2 cups (500 ml) chicken and duck or chicken stock

1 tsp salt, or to taste

1 tsp rice wine

1 tsp sesame oil

1/4 tsp MSG

1. Blanch the sea cucumbers in boiling water for one minute. Remove, clean, and cut into strips. Remove the prawns' heads, shell, and devein them. Wash and cut each in 2 lengthwise, parboil 1 minute, and drain. Cut the bamboo shoots into large slices. Cook the cellophane noodles in boiling water for 2 minutes, drain and rinse under cold running water. Slice the chicken meat, 1/8 inch (3 mm) thick.

2. Place noodles at the bottom of a fire pot. Arrange the sea cucumbers, prawns, chicken, bamboo shoot slices, and mushrooms on top.

3. Bring the stock to a boil in another pot. Add the salt, rice wine, MSG, and sesame oil. You may adjust the seasonings to taste. Pour into the fire pot.

4. Fill the chimney with burning charcoal. To serve, let diners help themselves to the ingredients as they boil in the pot. The ingredients are eaten by dipping them into soy sauce or other dips.

VEGETABLE AND

BEAN CURD DISHES

105. Spicy Fragrant Mung Bean Sprouts, Northeast China Style

1 lb (500 g) mung bean sprouts, with
roots removed
9 tbsp (100 ml) vegetable oil
10 whole Sichuan peppercorns
1 tsp scallions, shredded
4 dried or fresh hot red chili (chilli) peppers, seeded and shredded

1/2 tsp salt, or to taste
1/4 tsp vinegar
1/4 tsp sesame oil
3/4 oz (20 g) coriander (or cilantro), chopped in 1 inch (2 cm) sections
1/4 tsp MSG

1. Wash the bean sprouts and drain well.
2. Heat the oil in a wok until the oil surface ripples. Add the peppercorns and deep-fry until fragrant.
Scoop out and discard. Add the scallions and fry, add bean sprouts, red chili pepper shreds, and salt.
Stir-fry for 2 minutes. Pour in the vinegar and add MSG and sesame oil. Sprinkle with the coriander,
remove, and serve.

106. Stir-Fried Mung Bean Sprouts with Chives, Beijing-North China Style

9 oz (250 g) mung bean sprouts
2 eggs
2 oz (60 ml) vegetable oil
2 tsp salt, or to taste

2 oz (50 g) chives, washed thoroughly, cut in 1 1/4 inch (3 cm) sections
1/4 tsp MSG

1. Wash the bean sprouts well and remove the roots. Drain.
2. Beat the eggs. Heat 1 tbsp oil in a wok, and pour in the egg. Swirl the pan to make a very thin pancake. Cook until dry, then cut into shreds.
3. Heat the remaining 3 tbsp oil in a wok until the oil surface ripples. Add the salt and bean sprouts. Stir-fry for 2 to 3 minutes, or until the bean sprouts change colour. Add the chives and egg shreds. Stir-fry briefly, add the MSG, remove, and serve.

107. Stir-Fried Soy Bean Sprouts, Suzhou Style

1 lb (500 g) soy bean sprouts
5 tsp (30 ml) vegetable oil
1 tbsp soy sauce

1 tsp salt, or to taste
1/4 tsp sugar
1/4 tsp (1 g) vinegar

1. Wash the sprouts well and remove the roots. Drain.
2. Heat the oil in a wok until the surface ripples. Add the bean sprouts and stir-fry for 2 minutes. Add the soy sauce, salt, and 3 1/2 fl oz (100 ml) water. Cover the wok and simmer for 3 minutes. Uncover and sprinkle with vinegar and sugar. Stir, remove and serve.

108. Creamy Tomatoes, Hangzhou Style

9 oz (250 g) tomatoes
3 1/2 fl oz (100 ml) milk
2 tsp salt, or to taste

2 tbsp cornstarch (cornflour)
2 tsp melted chicken fat
1/4 tsp MSG

1. Blanch the tomatoes in boiling water for 30 seconds. Cut in half, squeeze out the seeds, and peel. Cut into six thin slices each and set aside.
2. Mix the milk, MSG, salt, and cornflour into a thick sauce.
3. Bring 5 oz (150 ml) of water to a boil in a pot or wok. Add the tomato slices and the sauce. Cook, stirring, until the sauce thickens. Sprinkle with the chicken fat and serve.

109. Stir-Fried Spinach, Shanghai Style

1 lb (500 g) spinach
10 tsp (50 ml) vegetable oil

4 1/2 tsp soy sauce or 2 tsp salt, or to taste
1 1/2 tsp sugar

1. Trim the spinach and wash well to remove all sand.
2. Heat 7 tsp of the oil in a wok until the oil surface ripples. Add the spinach and stir-fry for 1 minute, or until it just starts to wilt. Add the soy sauce, sugar and MSG. Stir in, then add the remaining 3 tsp of oil. Stir, remove, and serve.

110. Braised Creamed Cabbage, Tianjin Style

9 oz (250 g) hearts of white Chinese cabbage (*bok choy*)
4 tbsp (60 ml) vegetable oil
3 tbsp scallions, chopped
1 tsp rice wine
7 oz (200 ml) high stock (see p. 17)

3/4 tsp salt, or to taste
3 1/2 oz (100 ml) milk
2 tbsp cornstarch (cornflour) dissolved in 2
tbsp water
1/4 tsp sesame oil
1/4 tsp MSG

1. Wash the cabbage and cut into 5 inch by 1/2 inch (13cm by 10mm) strips. Stack cabbage in a wok with the white parts on the bottom. Add water to barely cover and simmer until soft. Remove, drain, and set aside.
2. Heat the oil in a wok until the oil surface ripples. Add the scallions and stir-fry until fragrant. Add the rice wine, stock, and salt. Bring to a boil and cook for 30 seconds. Add the cabbage and bring back to a boil. Turn down the heat and simmer 1 minute. Stir in the milk and MSG. Add the cornstarch-water mixture and cook, stirring, until thickened. Sprinkle with the sesame oil, remove, and serve.

111. Braised Chinese Cabbage with Shrimps, Northeast China Style

9 oz (250 g) Chinese cabbage (*bok choy*)
5 oz (150 ml) vegetable oil
1/2 tsp scallions, shredded
1/4 tsp fresh ginger, shredded
4 tsp dried shrimps, soaked
2 fresh or canned mushrooms, sliced
1 carrot, sliced thinly
5 oz (150 ml) clear stock (see p. 17)

2 tsp salt, or to taste
1 tsp soy sauce
1/8 tsp ground Sichuan peppercorn
2 tbsp cornstarch (cornflour) dissolved in 2 tbsp water
1/4 tsp sesame oil
1/4 tsp MSG

1. Wash the cabbage, drain well, and cut into 1 1/2 inch by 1 inch (4 cm by 2.5 cm) pieces.
2. Heat 3 tbsp of the oil in a wok until the surface ripples. Add the cabbage and stir-fry for 1 minute. Remove and set aside. Heat 7 tbsp of the oil. Add the scallions and ginger and stir-fry until fragrant. Add the cabbage, shrimps, mushroom and carrot. Pour in the stock and bring to a boil. Add the salt, soy sauce, and ground peppercorn. When the stock has been almost reduced, add the MSG and the cornstarch-water mixture. Cook, stirring, until thickened slightly. Add the sesame oil, remove, and serve.

112. Hot-and-Sour Cabbage, Beijing-North China Style

9 oz (250 g) cabbage
1 hot red chili (chilli) pepper
4 tbsp (50 ml) vegetable oil
1/2 tsp scallions, chopped
5 whole Sichuan peppercorns

3/4 tsp salt, or to taste
1 1/2 tsp vinegar
1 1/2 tsp sugar
1/4 tsp MSG

1. Wash the cabbage and cut into diamond-shaped pieces, 1 inch (3 cm) each side. Seed and dice the chili pepper.
2. Heat the oil in a wok until the oil surface ripples. Add the scallions, peppercorns and salt. Add the chili pepper and stir-fry for 30 seconds. Add cabbage and stir-fry 2 minutes. Stir in the vinegar, sugar and MSG. Remove and serve.

113. Quick Stir-Fried Cabbage, Sichuan Style

a large cabbage (*bok choy*) about 1 lb (500 g)
2 tbsp (30 ml) vegetable oil
4 dried hot red chili (chilli) peppers, whole but stems removed
15 whole Sichuan peppercorns
3/4 tsp salt, or to taste

1 tsp soy sauce
1 tsp sugar
1/2 tsp vinegar
2 tsp sesame oil
1/4 tsp MSG

1. Wash and drain the cabbage leaves.
2. Heat the oil in a wok until moderately hot. Add the chilis and peppercorns. Fry until browned and fragrant. Remove and discard peppercorns but reserve the liquid in a wok. Add the cabbage and stir-fry for a few seconds. Add the salt, soy sauce and sugar. Stir-fry until the cabbage leaves just start to wilt and are barely cooked. Sprinkle with the vinegar, remove cabbage and place in a dish, and let cool.
3. Seed and shred the chili peppers. Flatten the cabbage leaves and sprinkle with the chili shreds. Roll leaf into a small roll and cut crosswise, each into 1 1/4 inch (3cm) sections. Place in a dish: Mix the MSG and sesame oil with the wok liquid, pour over the cabbage rolls, and serve.

114. Marinated Cabbage, Suzhou Style

9 oz (250 g) cabbage
5 tsp soy sauce
1 tbsp sesame oil

1/4 tsp salt
1 1/2 tsp sugar

1. Wash the cabbage leaves and cut into 1 inch by 2 inch (3 cm by 5 cm) strips.
2. Place the cabbage in a pot of cold water and bring to a boil. Cook for 2 to 3 minutes, remove, and drain. Place in a bowl.
3. Mix the soy sauce, sesame oil, salt and sugar together, pour over the cabbage, and serve.

115. Soft-Fried Mushrooms, Sichuan Style

5 oz (150 g) reconstituted *koumo* mushrooms (substitute fresh or canned
mushrooms)
2 cups (500 ml) meat stock
1/4 tsp salt, or to taste
2 egg whites

5 1/2 tbsp (50g) flour
2 cups (500 ml) vegetable oil; uses
about 2 oz (60 ml)
spiced pepper-salt (see p. 10)
1/4 tsp MSG

1. Wash the mushrooms well to remove any sand. Remove the stems. Blanch twice in meat
stock, then drain and place in a bowl. Add the salt and MSG and mix well.
2. Whisk egg whites and flour into batter and coat the mushrooms.
3. Heat the oil in a wok to about 230°F (110°C), add the mushrooms one by one and deep-fry
until the batter is soaked with oil. Remove and drain. Heat the oil to 400°F (205°C), or until
a piece of scallion green or ginger browns quickly and a haze appears above the surface.
Deep-fry the mushrooms until brown. Mix well and serve with the spiced pepper-salt as a
dip.

116. Stir-Fried Green Peppers, Suzhou Style

9 oz (250 g) green peppers
4 tsp vegetable oil

3/4 tsp salt, or to taste
1/4 tsp sugar

1. Wash the peppers. Seed, remove the stems and cut into 1/2 inch (1 cm) squares.
2. Heat the oil in a wok over a high fire until the oil surface ripples. Add the peppers and stir-fry until they shrink slightly. Add the salt, sugar, and a little water. Stir-fry for 2 more minutes, and serve.

117. Deep-Fried Carrot Floss, Sichuan Style

1 lb (500 g) carrots

4 cups (1 litre) vegetable oil for deep-frying; uses about 3 1/2 oz (100 ml)

6 1/2 tbsp (100 g) sugar

1. Wash and shred the carrots.
2. Heat the oil in a wok to about 340°F (170°C), or until a piece of scallion green or ginger sizzles and moves around when tossed into the oil. Add the carrot shreds and deep-fry until they turn reddish-yellow. Remove and drain. Sprinkle with the sugar, and serve.

118. Marinated Carrot Shreds, Chengdu Style

9 oz (250 g) carrots
2 tsp salt, or to taste
1 tsp coriander (cilantro), chopped
1 tsp garlic shoot, shredded

5 tsp chili (chilli) oil
1 tsp sesame oil
1 1/2 tsp sugar
1 1/2 tsp vinegar

1. Wash and peel the carrots. Cut into 2 3/4 inch (7 cm) shreds. Mix with 1 tsp of the salt and place in a sieve or strainer so the excess water drains off.
2. Rinse the salt off and squeeze off the excess water. Place in a bowl with the coriander and garlic shoot. Add the chili oil, the remaining 1 tsp salt, the sesame oil, sugar and vinegar. Blend well and serve.

119. Marinated Three Shreds, Jiangsu Style

1 small fresh cucumber, about 7 oz (200 g)
3 1/2 oz (100 g) carrots
1 sheet *fenpi* (mung bean flour skin)
1/4 tsp salt , or to taste
5 tsp soy sauce

4 1/2 tsp sugar
2 tsp vinegar
1 1/2 tbsp (25g) fresh ginger, shredded
1 tbsp sesame oil
1/4 tsp MSG

1. Seed the cucumber. Cut into 1 1/2 inch (4 cm) shreds. Peel the carrot and shred. Dip the *fenpi* in boiling water and shred.
2. Mix the cucumbers and carrots with the salt and let marinate. Squeeze out the excess water and place on a serving dish. Add the *fenpi,* soy sauce, sugar, MSG, vinegar, and ginger, and blend well. Sprinkle with the sesame oil, and serve.

120. Deep-Fried Crisp Peanuts, Sichuan Style

1 lb (500 g) peanuts, shelled
2 tsp salt, or to taste
2 eggs

1 1/3 cups (200 g) cornstarch (cornflour)
4 cups (1 litre) vegetable oil; uses about
    3 1/2 fl oz (100 ml)

1. Place the peanuts in a sieve or colander and pour boiling water over them, stirring constantly. Then marinate in a bowl with 1 tsp salt.
2. Mix the eggs into a batter with half of the cornstarch and the remaining 1 tsp salt. Add the peanuts and coat well, then dust with the remaining cornstarch, shaking the bowl to separate the peanuts.
3. Heat the oil in a wok about 230°F (110°C). Add the peanuts and deep-fry until brown. Drain well, cool, and serve.

121. Sweet-and-Sour Shredded Lotus Roots, Hangzhou Style

1 lb (500 g) lotus roots
1 tbsp vegetable oil
5 whole Sichuan peppercorns
1 tsp soy sauce

1 tbsp vinegar
1 tbsp sugar
1 tsp cornstarch (cornflour) dissolved in 1 tsp water

1. Peel, wash, and shred the lotus roots.
2. Heat the oil in a wok until the oil surface ripples. Roast the peppercorns until brown, then discard. Add the lotus root shreds and stir-fry for 1 minute. Add the soy sauce, vinegar, sugar, and cornstarch mixture. Cook, stirring, until thickened. Remove and serve.

122. Braised Chinese Cabbage and Asparagus, Shandong Style

3 1/2 oz (100 g) fresh asparagus
10 1/2 oz (300 g) hearts of Chinese cabbage
  (*bok choy*)
3 tbsp vegetable oil
1/2 tsp scallions, chopped
1/2 tsp ginger, chopped
1 1/2 tsp rice wine

1/2 tsp salt, or to taste
1/2 cup (120 ml) chicken and duck broth or
  chicken broth
1 1/2 tbsp cornstarch (cornflour) dissolved
  in 1 1/2 tbsp water
3 tbsp melted chicken fat
1/2 tsp MSG

1. Peel the asparagus and cut crosswise into two sections. Wash the Chinese cabbage and separate the leaves. Blanch in boiling water for about 30 seconds. Remove, rinse in cold water, and drain well. Set aside.

2. Heat the oil in a wok until the oil surface ripples. Add the scallions and ginger, and stir-fry until fragrant. Add the rice wine, MSG, salt, and stock. Add the asparagus and cabbage and bring to a boil over high heat, then turn the fire to low and simmer for 3 to 5 minutes. Turn up the heat to high and add the cornstarch-water mixture. Cook, stirring, until thickened . Stir in the chicken fat, remove, and serve.

123. Crunchy Stir-Fried Kelp, Hangzhou Style

5 oz (150 g) dried broad-leafed kelp, soaked
8 tsp flour mixed with 4 tsp water
2 cups (500 ml) vegetable oil for deep-frying;
   uses about 2 1/2 oz (75 ml)
2 tsp soy sauce
1 tsp salt, or to taste
1 tbsp sugar

1 tbsp vinegar
1 tsp rice wine
1 tbsp garlic mash
1 tsp cornstarch (cornflour) dissolved in 1
   tbsp water
1 tsp sesame oil

1. Cut the kelp diagonally into slices. Coat with the flour batter.
2. Heat the oil in a wok to about 350°F (175°C), or until a piece of scallion green or ginger sizzles when tossed into the oil. Add the kelp and deep-fry until the batter hardens. Remove and drain. Heat the oil to 400°F (205°C), or until a scallion leaf browns quickly and a haze appears above the oil surface. Add the kelp and deep-fry until brown. Remove and drain well.
3. Pour all but 1 tbsp of the oil out of the wok. Heat until the oil surface ripples. Add the soy sauce, salt, sugar, vinegar, rice wine, and mashed garlic. Add the cornstarch mixture and the kelp. Cook, stirring, until the sauce thickens slightly. Add the sesame oil, remove, and serve.

124. Deep-Fried Potato Balls, Northeast China Style

1 lb (500 g) potatoes
1 tbsp (100 g) flour
1/4 tsp five-spice powder
5 tsp salt, or to taste
1/2 tsp scallions, chopped

1/2 tsp ginger, chopped
2 cups (500 ml) vegetable oil for deep-frying
1/4 tsp spiced pepper-salt (see p. 10)
1/4 tsp MSG

1. Wash and boil the potatoes, then peel and mash them. Mix well with the flour, five-spice powder, salt, MSG, scallions and ginger. Form into small balls. (see Illustration I)
2. Heat the oil in a wok to moderately hot, 230°F (110°C). Add the potato balls a few at a time and deep-fry until brown. (see Illustration II) Remove, drain and sprinkle with spiced pepper-salt.

125. Braised Eggplant, Beijing Style

9 oz (250 g) eggplants
9 oz (250 ml) vegetable oil for deep-frying;
  uses about 1 tbsp (15 ml)
1 tbsp soy sauce
1/2 tsp scallions, chopped
1/2 tsp salt

1/2 tsp fresh ginger, chopped
2 tbsp cornstarch (cornflour) dissolved in 2
  tbsp water
2 cloves garlic, peeled and crushed
1 tsp sesame oil

1. Peel the eggplant and cut into slices about 1/2 inch (1 cm) thick. Score the slices on one side about 1/8 inch (3 mm) deep and cut into 1 1/4 inch (3 cm) strips.
2. Heat the oil in a wok to 400°F (205°C) or until a piece of scallion green or ginger moves quickly when tossed into the oil and a haze appears above the oil surface. Add the eggplant and deep-fry until brown. Remove and drain well.
3. Blend the soy sauce, salt, scallions, ginger, the cornstarch-water mixture and 5 additional tsp water into a sauce.
4. Pour all but 2 tsp of the oil from the wok. Heat over high heat, until the oil surface ripples. Add the garlic and stir-fry until fragrant. Add the eggplant strips and the sauce. Bring to a boil and cook, stirring, until the sauce thickens. Sprinkle with the sesame oil, remove, and serve.

126. Mashed Eggplant, Beijing-Hebei Style

1 lb (500 g) eggplants
2 tsp sesame oil
2 tsp salt, or to taste
1 tbsp sesame paste

1/2 tsp fresh coriander (or cilantro), chopped
1/2 tsp chives, chopped
1 whole garlic, mashed

1. Peel the eggplant and cut into thin slices. Place in a heat-proof dish and steam for 20 minutes, or until very soft. Mash and let cool.
2. Mix well with the sesame oil, salt, sesame paste, coriander, chives, and garlic and serve.

127. Fried Bamboo Shoots, Jiangsu-Zhejiang Style

3/4 lb (350 g) fresh winter bamboo shoots
2 1/2 oz (75 g) *xuelihong* (preserved mustard green)

1 1/2 cups (350 ml) vegetable oil for deep-frying; uses about 2 oz (60 ml)
1/2 tsp MSG

1. Remove the husks from the bamboo shoots. Roll-cut into diamond-shaped chunks. Soak *xuelihong* in water for 5 minutes to reduce its saltiness. Squeeze out the excess water and cut into 1 1/2 inch (3.5 cm) pieces.

2. Heat the oil in a wok to about 400°F (205°C), or until a piece of scallion green or ginger browns quickly when tossed into the oil and a haze rises above the oil surface. Add *xuelihong* and deep-fry for 30 seconds. Remove and drain. Add the bamboo shoots and turn the heat to low. Deep-fry the bamboo shoots for 30 seconds, then raise the heat to high and deep-fry for 3 minutes, or until brown outside and tender inside. Remove and drain. Return *xuelihong* to the oil and deep-fry for 5 minutes. Remove and drain.

3. Pour all the oil out of the wok. Add *xuelihong* and bamboo shoots. Stir-fry to blend, then sprinkle with the MSG. Remove and serve.

128. Spicy Bean Curd, Sichuan Style

7 oz (200 g) fresh bean curd (*tofu*)
2 1/2 oz (75 g) lean boneless beef
2 1/2 oz (75 ml) vegetable oil
1/4 tsp salt, or to taste
1 tbsp fermented black beans, or hot soy bean paste
1 1/4 tsp ground hot red chili (chilli) pepper, without seeds

5 oz (150 ml) meat stock
1 tbsp garlic shoots, chopped (or use chopped garlic)
2 tsp soy sauce
1 tsp cornstarch (cornflour) dissolved in 1 tsp water
1/2 tsp ground Sichuan peppercorns
1/8 tsp MSG

1. Cut the bean curd into 3/4 inch (2 cm) cubes. Drop into boiling water for 1 minute. Remove and drain well. Mince the beef.
2. Heat the oil in a wok over high heat to moderately hot about 230°F (110°C). Add the beef and stir-fry until brown. Add the salt and fermented black beans. Stir-fry 1 minute. Add the ground chili pepper and stir-fry until fragrant. Add the stock and bean curd, bring to a boil and cook for 4 minutes. Keep the stock at a fast boil and add the garlic shoots or garlic, soy sauce and MSG. Stir in the cornstarch-water mixture and cook, stirring gently so as not to break the bean-curd cubes until thickened. Scoop out the bean curd and place in a serving dish. Sprinkle with the ground peppercorns, and serve.

129. Bean Curd Casserole, Beijing Style

7 oz (200 g) fresh bean curd (*tofu*)
2 oz (50 g) Chinese ham
5 oz (150 g) bamboo shoots, fresh or canned
7 oz (200 g) Chinese cabbage (*bok choy*)
6 cups (1,500 ml) chicken stock
2 tsp (10 g) dried shrimps, soaked and chopped
2 large sized (10 g) dried Chinese black mush-

rooms, reconstituted and sliced
1/2 tsp scallions, shredded
1/2 tsp fresh ginger, shredded
1 tbsp salt, or to taste
1 tsp melted chicken fat
1/4 tsp MSG

1. Slice the bean curd into thin triangles. Slice the Chinese ham, bamboo shoots and cabbage.
2. Lay the cabbage slices in the bottom of a casserole and pour in the stock. Put the bean curd on top of the cabbage. Then sprinkle with the shrimps, bamboo shoots, ham slices, black mushrooms, scallions, ginger, and salt. Bring to a boil over medium heat, then turn the heat to low and simmer for 15 minutes. Add the MSG and sprinkle with the chicken fat. Remove and serve.

130. Bean Curd Cocoons, Shanxi Style

1 lb (500 g) fresh bean curd (*tofu*)

2 eggs

1 tbsp salt, or to taste

9 oz (250 g) fresh shrimp

5 tsp sesame oil

1 tsp ginger, chopped

2 cups (500 ml) vegetable oil for deep-frying

5 fl oz (150 ml) clear stock (see p. 17)

1/2 tsp rice wine

1 tsp cornstarch dissolved in 1 tsp water

1/2 tsp MSG

1. Mash the bean curd and drain off any excess water. Place in a bowl with 1 egg, 2 1/2 tsp of the salt and 1/4 tsp of the MSG. Mix well. Set aside.

2. Shell the shrimps and mince them into a pulp. Mix with the sesame oil, the other egg, the remaining 1/2 tsp of salt, 1/4 tsp of the MSG and the ginger.

3. Spread bean curd on a clear surface. Mold it into small round pieces. To make the cocoons, take shrimp, and encase it in enough of the bean-curd mixture to make a cylinder about 1 1/2 inches long and 1/2 inch thick (4 cm by 7 mm). Continue until all the shrimp and bean curd are used.

4. Heat the oil in a wok to 420°F (220°C), or until a piece of scallion green or ginger browns quickly when tossed into the oil and a haze rises vigorously above the surface. Add the bean curd cocoons a few at a time and deep-fry until brown. Remove and drain well.

5. Pour the clear stock in a saucepan with the rice wine and the remaining salt and 1/4 tsp MSG. Bring to a boil. Add the cornstarch mixture and cook, stirring, until slightly thickened. Add the bean curd cocoons and stir gently to blend before serving.

131. Deep-Fried Bean Curd, Beijing Style

14 oz (400 g) fresh bean curd (*tofu*)
1/4 tsp scallions, chopped
1/4 tsp fresh ginger, chopped
1 tbsp salt, or to taste
1 tsp rice wine

3 cups (750 ml) vegetable oil for deep-frying;
  uses about 3 1/2 oz (100 ml)
2 tbsp (30 g) flour
2 eggs
1/4 tsp MSG

1. Cut the bean curd into 1/4 inch (6 mm) diamonds. Spread on a dish and sprinkle with the scallions, ginger, MSG, salt, and rice wine. Let marinate. Beat the eggs.
2. Heat the oil in a wok to about 210°F (100°C), or until small bubbles just appear around a piece of scallion green or ginger when tossed into the oil. Dip the bean curd into the flour and then into the egg. Add to the oil a few pieces at a time. Deep-fry until brown. Remove and drain well. Place in a dish. Garnish with cooked green leaves and serve.

132. Braised Bean Curd, Beijing Style

7 oz (200 g) fresh bean curd (*tofu*)
4 tsp soy sauce
1 tsp scallions, chopped
1 tsp ginger, chopped
1 tbsp flour
2 cups (500 ml) vegetable oil for
    deep-frying; uses about 2 oz
    (60 ml)
1 clove star anise
1 tsp salt, or to taste
1 tsp peppercorn oil
1 tsp garlic, chopped

1. Cut the bean curd into 1 1/4 inch squares by 1/4 inch thick (3 cm by 7 mm). Place in a bowl with 1 tbsp of the soy sauce, scallions, and ginger. Carefully mix the bean-curd squares with the flour (see Illustration I).
2. Beat the egg. Then pour the egg over the bean curd and blend well.
3. Heat the oil in a wok over high heat to very hot 350°F (180°C). Add the star anise, then add the bean curd, a few pieces at a time. Deep-fry until brown (see Illustration II). Remove the bean curd and star anise and drain well. Reserve the star anise.
4. Pour the oil out of the wok. Pour 1 cup (250 ml) of warm water, the remaining 1 tsp of soy sauce and the salt in the wok and bring to a boil. Add the bean curd and star anise. Bring back to a boil, then lower the heat and simmer for 10 minutes, or until the stock is reduced. Add the peppercorn oil and garlic. Remove and serve.

133. Bean Curd in Sauce, Shandong Style

1 lb (500 g) fresh bean curd (*tofu*)
2 oz (60 ml) vegetable oil
1 tsp dried shrimps, soaked and chopped
2 tsp sweet fermented flour sauce (substitute sweet bean paste or hoisin sauce)
1 tsp scallions, chopped
1 tsp fresh ginger, chopped
1 tsp garlic, chopped
3 1/2 oz (100 g) minced lean pork

5 tsp soy sauce
2 tsp rice wine
2 tsp fresh coriander (or cilantro), chopped
3 1/2 fl oz (100 ml) high stock (see p. 17)
1 tbsp cornstarch (cornflour) dissolved in tbsp water
3 tbsp (50 ml) peppercorn oil
1/2 tsp MSG

1. Place the bean curd in a heat-proof bowl and steam for 10 minutes. Remove, drain, and cut into 1/2 inch (1 cm) cubes (see Illustration I). Set aside.

2. Heat oil in a wok over high heat to just warm about 160°F (70°C). Add the shrimps, sweet fermented flour sauce, scallions, ginger, garlic, and pork. Stir-fry for 2 minutes. Add the soy sauce, rice wine, and stock. Stir and bring to a boil. Add the cornstarch-water mixture and cook, stirring, until the sauce thickens (see Illustration II). Pour over the bean curd. Add coriander and MSG, sprinkle with the peppercorn oil, and serve.

134. Bean Curd in Sesame Paste, Northeast China Style

9 oz (250 g) fresh bean curd (*tofu*)

2 tbsp sesame paste

1 1/2 tbsp fresh coriander (or cilantro), chopped

4 tsp salt, or to taste

1/4 tsp chili (chilli) oil

1. Cut the bean curd into 2 inch (5 cm) squares. Quick-boil in boiling water for 1 minute. Remove, drain, and place in a serving bowl.

2. Make a sauce by mixing the sesame paste with the salt and a little water. Pour over the bean curd and sprinkle with the chili oil and coriander and serve.

135. Bean Curd with Crab, Suzhou Style

12 oz (350 g) fresh bean curd (*tofu*)
2 oz (50 g) crab meat and eggs
4 1/2 tbsp (140 ml) vegetable oil
2 tsp scallions, chopped
5 tsp soy sauce
1/2 tsp salt, or to taste
2 tsp sugar

5 fl oz (150 ml) high stock (see p. 17)
1 tbsp cornstarch (cornflour) dissolved in 1 tbsp water
2 tsp rice wine
1/2 tsp ginger, chopped
1/8 tsp MSG

1. Cut the bean curd into 1/2 inch (1 cm) cubes.
2. Heat 3 tbsp of the oil in a wok until the oil surface ripples. Add 1 tsp of the scallions, the bean curd, soy sauce, 1/2 tsp of the salt, sugar, and 3 1/2 fl oz (100 ml) of the stock. Bring to a boil and simmer over low heat for 3 minutes. Turn the heat to high and add the MSG and 2 tsp of the cornstarch-water mixture. Cook, stirring, until thickened. Pour into a dish.
3. Heat the remaining 1 1/2 tbsp of oil until the surface ripples. Add the remaining 1 tsp of the scallions, the ginger, crab meat and eggs, and the remaining 1/4 tsp of salt. Stir-fry briefly and add the remaining 1 1/2 oz of stock. Bring to a boil and add the remaining of the cornstarch-water mixture. Cook, stirring, until thickened. Pour over the bean curd, and serve.

136. Bean Curd with Fresh Shrimps, Jiangsu Style

9 oz (250 g) fresh shrimps
5 oz (150 g) tomatoes
5 oz (150 g) bean curd
3 1/2 tbsp rice wine
1 tsp salt, or to taste
3 1/2 tbsp vegetable oil
10 1/2 oz (300 ml) high stock (see p. 17)

1/2 tsp scallions, chopped
1/2 tsp fresh ginger, chopped
2 1/2 tbsp cornstarch dissolved in 2 1/2 tbsp
   water
2 tsp sesame oil
1/4 tsp MSG

1. Remove the shrimps' heads. Shell, devein and wash the shrimps. Drain and mix with 5 tsp of the rice wine, 1/4 tsp of the MSG, and 1/2 tsp of the salt. Let stand.
2. Dip the tomatoes in boiling water for 30 seconds. Peel, seed and dice them. Dice the bean curd and place in a pot of cold water. Bring to a boil, remove the bean curd immediately, and drain.
3. Heat wok and add oil, the stock, the remaining salt and rice wine, the scallions, ginger, bean curd and shrimps. Bring to a boil. Add the tomatoes and 1/4 tsp MSG. Add the cornstarch-water mixture and cook, stirring gently. When the sauce returns to a boil, sprinkle with the sesame oil, remove, and serve.

SWEET DISHES

137. White Fungus with Rock Sugar, Sichuan Style

1/2 oz (15 g) white fungus (*tremella*)
1 1/8 cups (250 g) rock sugar or granulated
sugar

2 egg whites
20 tangerine sections, fresh or canned

1. Soak the white fungus in warm water for 1 hour. Remove the stems and clean thoroughly, discarding any discoloured parts. Break the clusters into individual pieces and let soak in a bowl of fresh water.

2. Heat 3 cups (750 ml) of water in a pot and add the sugar, letting it melt into a syrup. Beat the egg whites and mix them with a little water. Stir into the syrup and bring to a boil. Pour the syrup into a heat-proof bowl and add the white fungus. Cover the bowl tightly, place in a steamer, and steam for 1 1/2 hours or until the white fungus are very soft and the liquid is thick. Pour into individual bowls and place tangerines on top of the soup. Serve warm or chilled.

138. Tangerine Duff, Kaifeng Style

3 tangerines
7 tbsp (100g) sugar
5 tbsp cornstarch (cornflour) dissolved in 5

tbsp water
2 oz (50g) haw jelly, diced

1. Peel the tangerines and divide into sections. Remove the strings and seeds and cut into 1/2 inch (1 cm) dice. Set aside.
2. Pour 5 cups (1,250 ml) of water into a saucepan. Add the sugar and bring to a boil. Skim off the foam. Add the cornstarch and cook, stirring, until slight'y thickened. Stir in the tangerines. Pour into individual bowls and sprinkle with the diced haw jelly.

139. Peaches in Syrup, Kaifeng Style

1 1/2 lb (750 g) peaches   2 tbsp (50 g) honey
10 tbsp (100 g) sugar or to taste

1. Halve the peaches and remove the pits. Place in a heat-proof bowl and steam until tender and cooked through. Peel and cut each half in half again. Let cool.
2. Bring 5 cups (1,250 ml) of water to a boil. Stir in the sugar and honey and boil until the syrup thickens. Pour over the peaches, let cool slightly, and serve.

140. Chinese Yams in Syrup, Beijing Style

1 1/2 lb (750 g) Chinese yams
1 1/3 cups (300 g) sugar
2 tbsp (50 g) honey
1 tbsp preserved osmanthus flowers (optional)

2 oz (50g) cucumber, diced
2 oz (50 g) haw jelly, diced
1 tbsp sesame oil

1. Wash and peel the yams and cut into 1 inch (26 mm) sections. Set aside.
2. Heat the oil and 3 1/2 tbsp (50 g) sugar in a wok over a low fire, stirring until melts into a yellow syrup. Stir in the yam sections. Add 3 cups (750 ml) of water, the remaining 1 cup (250g) sugar, the honey and the osmanthus flowers. Simmer over low heat until the yam is very tender and the syrup thickens. Place in a dish, sprinkle with the haw jelly and cucumber dice, and serve.

141. Apples in Spun Syrup, Jiangsu Style

1 lb (500 g) firm, slightly tart apples
1 egg
3 1/2 oz or 11 tbsp (100 g) flour
2 cups (500 ml) vegetable oil for deep-frying;

uses about 4 1/2 oz (130 ml)
1/2 cup (125g) rock sugar or granulated sugar
1 tbsp sesame oil

1. Peel the apples and cut into diamond-shaped pieces or wedges. Mix the egg and flour into a batter. Coat the apple pieces with the batter.
2. Heat the oil in a wok to about 350°F (175°C), or until a sliver of ginger or a piece of green leaf sizzles when tossed into the oil. Add the apple pieces and deep-fry for 1 minute or until the pieces float to the surface. Remove and drain well.
3. Pour all the oil out of the wok. Add 1 cup of boiling water and the rock sugar. Bring to a boil, then turn the heat to low and cook, stirring constantly, until the syrup spins a thread. Add the apple pieces. Turn and toss carefully so each piece is covered with the syrup. Remove and serve immediately, before· the syrup hardens. Sprinkle with the sesame oil. Dip each piece of apple into a bowl of cold water to make it cool enough to eat.

142. Tomatoes in Sugar Syrup, Sichuan Style

6 ripe tomatoes, about 1 1/2 lb (750 g), of
    uniform size
1 egg white

7 oz (200 g) rock sugar or 14 tbsp granu-
    lated sugar

1. Dip the tomatoes in boiling water for a few seconds, then peel, quarter and seed. Beat the egg white
with 2 oz (50 ml) water.
2. Melt the rock sugar in a saucepan of 1 1/2 cups boiling water. Discard impurities. Add the egg
white and boil until the syrup thickens. Let cool, pour over the tomatoes, and serve.

143. Stuffed Apples, Beijing Style

1 lb (500 g) large apples, of uniform size
3 1/2 oz (100 g) glutinous rice
6 tbsp (85g) sugar
2 tbsp cornstarch (cornflour) dissolved in 2 tbsp water
1/2 oz (15 g) walnut meat
1/2 oz (15 g) melon seeds, skinned

1/2 oz (15 g) raisins
1/2 oz (15 g) preserved green plum, diced
1/2 oz (15 g) preserved dates, pitted
1/2 oz (15 g) preserved melon strips
1/2 oz (15 g) preserved tangerine, diced
1/2 oz (15 g) preserved apple, diced
1/2 oz (15 g) haw jelly, diced

1. Wash the apples and cut off the tops 1 1/4 inches (3cm) below the stems. These will be the caps. Peel and core the apples (see Illustration I).
2. Wash the glutinous rice until the water is clear and drain. Put into a heat-proof bowl. Add 1/2 cup (130 ml) water. Steam for 25 minutes. Mix rice with the walnut meat, melon seeds, raisins, preserved green plums, dates, melon strips, tangerines, apple, and 4 tbsp sugar (see Illustration II).
3. Fill the apples and top with the caps (see illustration III). Fasten the caps on with toothpicks. Place in a heat-proof dish and steam for 20 minutes, or until tender.
4. Remove the toothpicks and place the apples in serving dishes.
5. Bring 1 cup of water and the remaining 2 tbsp sugar to a boil in a saucepan. Add the cornstarch, stirring, until slightly thickened. Pour over the apples. Sprinkle with the diced haw jelly, and serve.

144. Chinese Yams in Spun Syrup, Shandong Style

1 lb (500 g) Chinese yams (or sweet potatoes) uses about 2 1/2 oz (75 ml)
3 cups (750 ml) vegetable oil for deep-frying; 5/8 cup (150 g) sugar

1. Wash, peel and roll-cut the yams into pieces. Soak in boiling hot water and remove immediately. Drain well (see Illustration I).
2. Heat the oil in a wok over medium heat to about 250°F (120°C), or until small bubbles appear around a piece of green leaf tossed into the oil. Add the yams and deep-fry until cooked or brown. Remove and drain (see Illustration II).
3. Pour all but 2 tbsp of the oil out of the wok. Turn the heat to low and add the sugar, stirring constantly until it dissolves. Cook until the syrup caramelizes and turns light brown. Immediately add the yams and remove wok from the heat. Quickly toss the yam pieces so they are well-coated with the syrup, which will spin a thread. Place on a plate and serve immediately. Dip each piece in cold water to cool it enough to eat.

145. Three Fruits in Syrup, Shandong Style

9 oz (250 g) haws (hawthorn fruits, or use fresh crab apples)

9 oz (250 g) fresh chestnuts (or use canned peeled whole chestnuts)

9 oz (250 g) canned ginkgo nuts

2 1/2 tbsp sesame oil

2 tbsp (25 g) sugar

2 tbsp honey

1 tsp osmanthus flower syrup (optional)

1. Wash the haws and simmer in water until partially cooked. Drain, then core, peel, and wash the haws. If using fresh chestnuts, wash them and cut a cross through their pointed ends and a third of the way down the nuts. Plunge into boiling water for 1 minute, remove, drain, and shell. Then let them soak in warm water for about 30 minutes and remove the inner peels.
2. Put the chestnuts in a heat-proof bowl. Cover with water and steam for 20 minutes, or until soft.
3. Pour 1 1/4 tbsp of the sesame oil into a wok and heat. Add the sugar and cook, stirring constantly, until the syrup turns light brown. Slowly add 9 oz (250 ml) water, the honey, haws, chestnuts, and ginkgo nuts. Bring to a boil, then turn the heat to low and simmer until the syrup thickens. Stir in the osmanthus flower syrup and the remaining 1 1/4 tbsp sesame oil, and serve.

146. Sweet Potatoes in Syrup, Kaifeng Style

1 lb (500 g) sweet potatoes
2 cups (500 ml) vegetable oil for deep-frying; uses about 3 1/2 oz (100 ml)
5/8 cup or 10 1/2 tbsp (150 g) sugar

2 tbsp (50 g) honey
2 tbsp cornstarch (cornflour), dissolved in 2 tbsp water
2 oz (50 g) haw jelly, diced

1. Wash and peel the sweet potatoes. Cut into 2 1/2 by 3/4 inch by 3/4 inch (6 cm by 2 cm by 2 cm) strips.
2. Heat the oil in a wok to 350°F (175°C), or until a 1-inch (25 mm) cube of day-old bread browns in 1 minute when dropped into the oil. Add the sweet potatoes, and deep-fry until brown. Remove and drain (see Illustration I).
3. Pour out the oil and add 9 oz (250 ml) of water to the wok. Add the sugar and cook, stirring, until it dissolves. Then add the honey and cornstarch. Cook, stirring, until thickened. Add the sweet potatoes and stir so each piece is coated with the syrup. Place on a plate, sprinkle with the haw jelly, and serve.

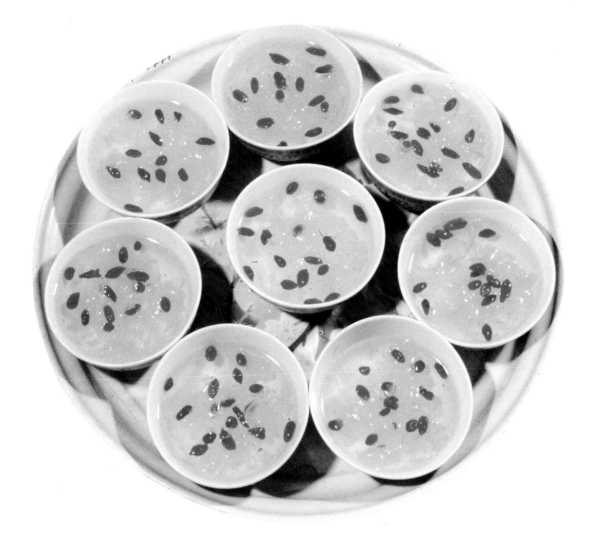

147. Chinese Wolfberries and White Fungus, Beijing Style

1/2 oz (15 g) white fungus (*tremella*)
1/6 oz (5 g) Chinese wolfberries
1 egg white, beaten

5/8 cup (150 g) rock sugar or granulated sugar
3 1/2 tbsp (50 g) granulated sugar

1. Soak the white fungus in warm water for 1 hour. Rinse, remove the stems, and cut away any discoloured or hard parts. Wash wolfberries and drain.
2. Bring 8 cups of water to a boil in a large pot. Add the beaten egg white, rock sugar and sugar, stirring constantly. Skim off any foam and continue boiling until the water turns clear. Add the white fungus and wolfberries and return to a boil. Cover the pot and simmer over low heat for 1 to 1 1/2 hours. Remove and serve.
Note: An early version of this dish dates back to the Tang Dynasty (618-907A.D.). It used to be served at imperial banquets, and is thought to be a tonic for the eyes and lungs.

148. Lotus Seeds in Sugar Syrup, Beijing-Hebei Style

7 oz (200 g) dried lotus seeds, skinned and
  bitter germ removed
1/4 cup (50 g) rock sugar or granulated sugar

7 tbsp (100 g) granulated sugar
1 oz (25 g) haw jelly, diced

1. Wash the lotus seeds and place in a heat-proof bowl with water to just cover. Steam until the seeds are very soft. Reserve the water in the bowl. Drop the seeds in boiling water for 10 seconds. Remove, drain, and set aside.
2. Pour 1/2 cup of the steaming water into a pot and add fresh water, if needed, to make up the amount. Add the rock sugar and granulated sugar and bring to a boil. Immediately pour over lotus seeds. Sprinkle with the haw jelly cubes and serve.

149. Creamy *Baihe*, Jiangxi Style

14 oz (400 g) fresh *baihe*, a plant related to the lily family; the dried white petals are eaten
7 oz (200 ml) milk

5 tbsp (75 g) sugar
2 tsp sesame oil
2 tbsp cornstarch (cornflour) dissolved in 2 tbsp water

1. Break the flower petals off the stems and wash. Blanch the petals twice in boiling water and drain.
2. Pour the milk into a wok and add the sugar, sesame oil, flower petals, and cornstarch. Heat the wok, bring to a boil and stir for several times and remove. The cooking must be done quickly and carefully to prevent the dish from sticking to the wok.

150. Sweet Marinated Lotus Roots, Shandong Style

14 oz (400 g) fresh lotus roots
7 tbsp (100 g) granulated sugar
1/4 tsp green preserved plum, shredded (substitute candied green cherry)
1/4 tsp red preserved plum, shredded (substitute candied red cherry)

1. Wash and peel the lotus roots. Remove the joints and cut into 1/4 inch (1/2 cm) slices.
2. Blanch in boiling water for 1 minute, rinse under cold water and drain well. Place on a serving dish and sprinkle with the sugar and the preserved plums or cherries.
Note: This easily-prepared dish of crunchy lotus roots is a popular summer refreshment.

151. Deep-Fried Watermelon, Beijing-Hebei Style

1 watermelon, about 10 lb
7 tbsp (100 g) cornflour
11 tbsp (100 g) flour
2 egg whites, beaten
7 tbsp cornstarch (cornflour)
3 cups (750 ml) vegetable oil for deep-frying;
  uses about 3 1/2 oz (100 ml)

1. Cut the watermelon in half and scoop out the pulp.
Remove any seeds from the pulp and cut the pulp into
diamonds. Coat with the flour. Mix the egg whites
with cornstarch and a little water into a batter.
2. Heat the oil in a wok over high fire to about 250°F
(120°C), or until small bubbles appear around a 1 inch
(2 cm) cube of day-old bread dropped into the oil.
Dip the watermelon pieces in the batter and add to
the oil. Deep-fry until the coating becomes firm. Turn
off the heat and continue to deep-fry the watermelon
until light brown. Remove, drain well, sprinkle with
the sugar, and serve.

152. Watermelon with Sauce, Beijing Style

4 1/2 lb (2 kg) watermelon
7/8 cup (200 g) granulated sugar
4 tsp osmanthus flowers (or use candied rose
or violet petals)
2 drops red flavouring colour (red food col-

ouring)
8 tbsp cornstarch (cornflour) dissolved in 8
tbsp water
1 oz (25 g) haw jelly, cubed

1. Halve and seed the watermelon and cut the pulp into small cubes. Set aside.
2. Heat 4 1/2 cups (1 litre) water in a pot. Add the sugar and osmanthus flowers and bring to a boil, stirring, until the sugar dissolves. Skim off any foam. Add the red flavouring colour and cornstarch. Cook, stirring until the sauce becomes a thin glaze. Remove and let stand until cool. Place the watermelon and haw jelly cubes on a serving dish, cover with the sauce, and serve.

153. Syrup-Coated Peanuts, Beijing-Hebei Style

1 lb (500 g) peanuts
5/8 cup (150 g) granulated sugar

10 tsp (50 g) cornflour

1. Heat the peanuts in a wok or pan. Dry-fry them until very crisp. Set aside.
2. Heat the sugar and 3 1/2 oz (100 ml) warm water in a wok, stirring until the sugar dissolves.
Continue to stir until the thin syrup bubbles. Stir in the peanuts. Gradually add the cornflour until the
peanuts are well-coated with the syrup. Remove, let cool slightly, and serve.

SOUPS

154. Sparerib Soup, Wuhan Style

9 oz (250 g) pork spareribs
5 tsp vegetable oil
3/4 tsp salt, or to taste
1/2 tsp fresh ginger, chopped

1 tsp scallions, chopped, white parts only
1/8 tsp rice wine
1/4 tsp MSG

1. Wash the spareribs and chop into 1 inch by 2 inch (3 cm × 5 cm) pieces.
2. Heat the oil in a wok over high heat until the oil surface ripples. Add the spareribs and stir-fry for 10 minutes, or until the ribs turn a lighter colour and give off most of their juices. Place in a heavy casserole with the salt and ginger. Add 2 1/2 cups (600 ml) of water, cover and bring to a boil. Boil for 2 hours·over high heat, replenishing the water if necessary. Add the MSG and scallions. Turn down the heat and simmer for 30 minutes. Remove and serve.

155. Egg-Drop Soup, Chengdu Style

2 eggs, beaten
5 tbsp wood ears, soaked
2 oz (50 g) hearts of Chinese cabbages
2 1/2 tbsp vegetable oil or lard

1/2 tbsp sesame oil
2 cups (500 ml) clear stock (see p. 17)
3/4 tsp salt, or to taste
1/4 tsp MSG

1. Wash and slice the wood ears and cabbage hearts.
2. Heat 2 1/2 tbsp of the vegetable oil or lard in a wok. Add the eggs and fry until browned on both sides. Remove and cut into small pieces. Set aside. Pour the stock into the wok and add the salt, wood ears, cabbage hearts , eggs, and MSG. Bring to a boil and let boil 1 minute. Sprinkle with the 1/2 tbsp sesame oil, and serve.

156. Chicken Velvet Soup, Sichuan Style

4 1/2 oz (125 g) boneless chicken breast
4 egg whites
2 1/2 tsp cornstarch (cornflour)
1 1/2 tsp salt, or to taste
1/2 tsp pepper

4 cups (1 litre) clear stock (see p. 17)
2 oz (50 g) Chinese cabbage hearts
1 tsp Chinese ham, chopped
3/4 tsp MSG

1. Use the upper edge of a cleaver to chop the chicken breast into a paste or a velvet, or use a food processor. Place in a bowl.
2. Beat the egg whites lightly and mix with the cornstarch. Add a little water to the chicken and stir to separate the chicken flesh. Stir in the egg white mixture, 1 tsp of the salt, 1/2 tsp of the MSG, the pepper, and 1/4 cup (60 ml) of the stock, 1 ingredient at a time. Stir into a paste.
3. Pour the stock into a saucepan and heat to boiling. Add the remaining 1/4 tsp MSG and 1/2 tsp salt. Then stir in the chicken paste and return to a boil, then turn the heat to low and simmer for 10 minutes, or until the chicken paste turns white and resembles very soft bean curd puree.
4. Blanch the cabbage hearts briefly in boiling water and rinse in cold water. Drain and cut each crosswise into two halves. Place in a large soup tureen. Add the chicken soup. Sprinkle with the chopped ham, and serve.

157. Egg Bubble Soup, Beijing-Hebei Style

4 (250 g) eggs, beaten
3 1/2 oz (100 g) lard or vegetable oil
1 1/2 tsp salt, or to taste

1/8 tsp pepper
1 tsp scallions, chopped
1 tsp MSG

Heat the oil in a wok over low heat to about 350°F (175°C), or until a piece of scallion green sizzles and moves around when dropped in the oil. Add the eggs and fry until the egg solution bubbles but has not yet begun to brown. Add 4 cups (1 litre) of water. Stir in the salt, MSG, and pepper. Simmer until fragrant. Pour the soup into a tureen, sprinkle with the scallions, and serve.

158. Walnut Porridge, Jiangsu Style

7 oz (200 g) walnuts
2 oz (50 g) red dried dates (*jujubes*, optional)

2 oz (50 g) rice
7/8 cup (200 g) sugar

1. Soak the walnuts in water, then skin and rinse in cold water. Simmer the dates in water until plump, then remove the skins and pits of dates. Wash the rice and soak in warm water for 2 hours.
2. Mince the walnuts and dates, then mix with the rice and enough water to make a paste. Grind until very fine and smooth, in a grinder or in a food processor.
3. Pour the paste in a saucepan. Add the sugar and 2 cups (500 ml) of water. Heat to boiling, and stir constantly until the paste becomes as thick as cornmeal. Remove and serve in bowls.

159. White Fungus Soup, Shandong Style

1/3 oz (10 g) white fungus (*tremella*)
3 cups (750 ml) clear stock (see p. 17)
1 tsp soy sauce

1/4 tsp salt, or to taste
1 tbsp rice wine
1/4 tsp MSG

1. Wash the white fungus in warm water, drain and place in a bowl with 2 cups (500 ml) of boiling water. Cover the bowl and let the white fungus soak for 15 minutes, or until soft. Drain and remove the stems and any hard or discoloured parts. Wash in warm water three times, then soak again in boiling water for 3 minutes. Remove and place in a tureen.
2. Pour the stock in a saucepan and add the soy sauce and salt. Heat over high heat to boiling and skim off any foam. Stir in the rice wine and MSG. Ladel 1 cup (250 ml) of the stock over the fungi and let soak for 10 minutes. Drain. Then reheat the remaining 2 cups (500 ml) of stock, add to the tureen, and serve.
Note: In this dish, the white fungus are tender and nutritious and the soup delicately flavoured.

160. Soy Bean Soup with Pork Cubes, Shandong Style

3 1/2 oz (100 g) lean boneless pork, cubed
3 1/2 oz (100 g) soy beans, cooked
3 1/2 oz (100 ml) vegetable oil
2 tsp scallions, shredded
2 tsp fresh ginger, shredded

2 tsp soy sauce
1/4 tsp salt, or to taste
4 cups (1 litre) clear stock (see p. 17)
1/2 tsp MSG

Heat the oil in a wok until the oil surface ripples. Add the scallions and ginger and stir-fry until fragrant. Add the pork cubes. Stir-fry until the pork turns white. Stir in the soy sauce and salt. Add the soy beans and stock. Bring to a boil, skim off any foam, and add the MSG. Remove and serve.

161. White Gourd Soup with Dried Shrimps, Beijing-Hebei Style

9 oz (250 g) white gourd
1 cup (250 ml) high stock (see p. 17)
1 tbsp dried shrimps, soaked
3/4 tsp salt

1/4 tsp scallions, chopped
2 tsp sesame oil
1/4 tsp MSG

1. Cut white gourd into 2 inch by 2 inch by 1/4 inch (5 cm by 5 cm by 7 mm) slices.
2. Bring the high stock to a boil and add the white gourd slices, shrimps and salt. Simmer for 20 minutes, or until the white gourd is cooked. Sprinkle with the scallions, MSG, and sesame oil. Remove and serve.

162. Muxi Soup, Northeast China Style

5 oz (150 g) lean boneless pork
2 spinach
1 tbsp (5 g) wood ears, soaked
2 eggs, beaten
4 cups (1 litre) clear stock (see p. 17)

1 tbsp soy sauce
1/2 tsp salt
1 tsp peppercorn water
4 tsp sesame oil
1/4 tsp MSG

1. Cut the pork into fine slivers. Wash the spinach well, drain, and cut into 1 1/4 inch (3 cm) slices. Blanch in boiling water briefly and drain. Break the wood ears into small pieces.
2. Heat the stock in a pot. Add the pork, wood ears, soy sauce, salt, and peppercorn water and bring to a boil. Pour in the eggs in a steady stream, stirring the stock with a circular motion so the egg covers the surface. Add the MSG. Sprinkle the sesame oil and the spinach on top. Remove and serve.

163. Chinese Cabbage Soup with Dried Shrimps, Shandong Style

10 1/2 oz (300 g) hearts of Chinese cabbage
  (*bok choy*)
3 tbsp (50 g) dried shrimps, soaked
2 tsp Chinese ham, sliced

2 Chinese black mushrooms, soaked
2 cups (500 ml) high stock (see p. 17)
1/2 tsp salt, or to taste
1 tsp melted chicken fat

1. Cut cabbage hearts into 1/2 inch by 1 1/4 inch (1 cm by 3cm) strips. Blanch briefly in boiling water and drain. Halve the mushrooms and discard the stems.
2. Pour the stock into a pot and add the ham, mushrooms, shrimps, cabbage, and salt. Bring to a boil and skim off any foam. Simmer until the cabbage hearts are very tender. Pour into a tureen, sprinkle with the chicken fat, and serve.

164. Hot-and-Sour Beef Soup, Jiangsu Style

5 oz (150 g) lean boneless beef
1 tsp salt, or to taste
5 tsp rice wine
2 tbsp cornstarch (cornflour) dissolved in 2 tbsp water
1 small carrot, about 3 1/2 oz (100 g)
2 tbsp vegetable oil

2 1/2 cups (600 ml) high stock (see p. 17)
1 oz (25 g) cellophane noodles, cut into 4 inch (10 cm) long, soaked in cold water until soft
1 1/2 tbsp vinegar
2 tsp fresh coriander (or cilantro), chopped
1 tbsp chili (chilli) oil
1/4 tsp MSG

1. Wash the beef and cut into slivers. Mix with 1/2 tsp of the salt, 2 tsp of the rice wine, and 1 tbsp of the cornstarch. Wash and peel the carrot and cut into slivers.

2. Heat the oil in a wok until the oil surface ripples. Add the carrot slivers and stir-fry briefly. Add the stock, cellophane noodles, and 1/2 tsp of the salt, and bring to a boil. Add the beef slivers, 1 tbsp rice wine, vinegar, MSG, the remaining cornstarch-water mixture, and coriander. Return to the boil and pour into a tureen. Sprinkle with the chili oil and serve.

RICE, NOODLES
AND DUMPLINGS

165. Noodles with Fried Bean-Paste Sauce, Beijing-North China Style

1 lb (500 g) flour noodles
9 oz (250 g) lean and fat pork, minced
5 tsp (25 g) sweet fermented flour paste
(sweet bean sauce or hoisin sauce)
5 peppercorns
5 tbsp vegetable oil

1 tsp scallions, chopped
1 tsp fresh ginger, chopped
5 tbsp soy sauce
1 1/2 tsp salt, or to taste
1 cup (200 ml) clear stock (see p. 17)
1 tbsp cornstarch dissolved in 1 tbsp water

1. Add enough water to the bean paste sauce to make a thin paste. Heat oil in a wok until the oil surface ripples. Add peppercorns and deep-fry until fragrant. Remove and discard peppercorns. Add the pork, the scallions, ginger, soy sauce, salt and the paste. Stir-fry for about 1 minute, then add the stock and cornstarch. Bring to a boil and cook, stirring, until thickened. Transfer to a serving bowl.
2. Bring a pot of water to a boil and add the noodles. Bring back to a boil and let cook for 30 seconds. Add cold water two or three times, each time bringing the water back to the boil until the noodles are just cooked. Drain in a colander and place on dishes or in bowls. Diners help themselves to some of the sweet bean paste, starting with about 1 tbsp and adding more to taste.

166. Peddler's Hot and Spicy Noodles (*Dandan Noodles*), Sichuan Style

1 lb (500 g) flour noodles
4 tbsp sesame paste
5 tsp sesame oil
5 oz (150 ml) soy sauce
3 tbsp vegetable oil or lard

5 tsp scallions, chopped
2 oz (50 g) Sichuan preserved cabbage, chopped, or fresh coriander (or cilantro)
5 tbsp chili (chilli) oil
1 tsp MSG

1. Mix the sesame paste with the sesame oil and set aside. Mix together the soy sauce, vegetable oil or lard, scallions, preserved cabbage or coriander, MSG, and chili oil, and divide among 5 serving bowls.
2. Bring a pot of water to a boil and add the noodles. Bring back to a boil and let cook for 30 seconds. Add enough cool water to stop the boiling, then bring back to the boil. Add more cool water and bring to a boil a third time. This time, boil until the noodles are just cooked. Drain well in a colander and divide among the 5 bowls. Blend the noodles with the seasonings, and serve.

167. Stir-Fried Noodles with Chicken, Beijing-North China Style

1 lb (500 g) flour noodles

10 1/2 oz (300 g) boneless chicken breast, skinned

1 egg white

2 1/2 tbsp cornstarch (cornflour) dissolved in 1 1/4 tbsp water

13 tbsp (200 ml) vegetable oil (or lard)

7 oz (200 g) chives, washed well and cut into 1 inch (3 cm) sections

1 tbsp salt, or to taste

1 cup (200 ml) chicken broth

1/4 tsp MSG

1. Shred the chicken breasts. Mix the egg white and the cornstarch-water into a paste and coat the chicken shreds.

2. Heat 4 1/2 tbsp (l00 ml) of the oil in a wok to about 212°F (100°C). Add the chicken shreds and cook, stirring, until they turn white. Pour out the oil and set it aside. Mix the chives, MSG, salt, and stock with the chicken and bring to a boil. Drain off and reserve the broth and seasonings. Place the chicken shreds in a bowl (see Illustration I).

3. Boil the noodles 3 times, as described in recipes 165 and 166. After the final boiling, rinse in cold water and drain well.

4. Heat 4 1/2 tbsp (100 ml) of the oil, including that used earlier, in the wok until the oil surface ripples. Tilt the wok to swirl the oil around. Add the noodles in an even layer. Shallow-fry them, swirling the wok so they cook evenly. Fry until browned on one side, then slide the wok scoop or a spatula under the noodles and turn them over. Sprinkle the other 4 tbsp of oil around the edges and shallow-fry the noodles until browned on the other side (see Illustration II). Add the reserved chicken broth. Cover the wok and simmer for 1 minute, or until the noodles absorb the sauce. Toss the noodles with chopsticks or a fork and add the chicken shreds. Stir, remove, and serve.

168. "Crossing the Bridge" Noodles, Yunnan Style

9 oz (250 g) very fine Chinese egg noodles
1 oz (25 g) spinach or rape
2 oz (50 g) boneless chicken breast
2 oz (50 g) fish filet, skinned
2 oz (50 g) shrimps or prawns, shelled
1/2 tsp rice wine

1/8 tsp fresh ginger, chopped
1/8 tsp salt, or to taste
1/8 tsp soy sauce
6 cups (1,500 ml) chicken broth
5 tbsp chicken fat
1/2 tsp MSG

1. Blanch the spinach or rape briefly in boiling water, drain, and set aside. Mix the rice wine, ginger, 1/8 tsp of the salt, and the soy sauce into a marinade. Slice the chicken, fish, and prawns paper-thin. Spread out on a serving platter and add the marinade. Let stand.

2. Heat a pot of water to boiling and add the noodles. Bring back to a boil and cook uncovered until they are soft, about 4 minutes for dried noodles and 2 minutes for fresh ones. Drain in a colander and lay the vegetable on top.

3. Bring the chicken broth to a boil in a saucepan and add the MSG, the remaining 1/2 tsp of salt, and the chicken fat. Bring to a fast boil for 1 minute. Transfer to a tureen and bring to the table with the platter of meats and the colander of noodles.

4. Pour the meat and noodles into the boiling hot broth. They will cook instantly. Stir and serve in individual bowls.

Note: The noodles poured from one bowl to another bowl of boiling hot broth is like a bridge. Hence the name of the dish.

169. Shrimp Noodles, Guangdong Style

1 1/2 tsp salt, or to taste
high stock (see p. 17) or hotbed leek
  sauce (see below)
4 1/2 cups (500 g) flour, sifted
5 oz (150 g) shrimp, shelled and deveined
4 egg whites

1. Mince the shrimp into a pulp and mix with the egg whites, salt, and flour. Add enough water to knead a smooth, elastic dough. Roll out into a very thin sheet and fold into 3 layers. Cut crosswise into fine noodles.
2. Heat 5 cups (1,250 ml) of water to boiling and add the noodles. Bring back to a boil and cook uncovered until the noodles are done, about 1 1/2 minutes.
3. Serve the noodles in bowls with high stock or hotbed leek sauce, made by boiling leek, lard, oyster sauce together and thickening the sauce by adding dissolved cornflour.

170. Sautéed Dumplings, Henan Style

For the dough:
4 1/2 cups (500 g) flour, sifted
4 1/2 tsp baking powder
For the filling:
7 oz (200 g) boneless mutton, minced
4 tsp salt, or to taste
1 lb (500 g) turnips, cooked and chopped
3 1/2 oz (100 g) scallions, chopped
1 tsp fresh ginger, chopped
1 tsp five-spice powder
5 tbsp sesame oil
1 tbsp soy sauce
1 tsp MSG

1. Mix the flour and baking powder with 9 oz (250 ml) of water. Knead until smooth and elastic, then cover with a warm wet cloth and let rise.
2. Place mutton in a bowl with 5 oz (150 ml) of water and the salt. Stir in one direction until it becomes a paste. Mix the turnips and scallions together and mince. Squeeze off any excess water and add to the mutton. Stir in the MSG, ginger, five-spice powder, 2 tbsp of the sesame oil, and the soy sauce, and mix well.
3. Knead dough for three minutes. Divide the dough into 4 pieces. Divide the pieces into 3/4 inch or 12 g balls. Divide the filling into as many portions as there are dough balls. Roll the balls into flat circles about 3 inches (7 to 8 cm) in diameter. Place some filling in the centre of each round and pinch the edges together to make a dumpling. Repeat until all the filling is used.
4. Heat 1 tsp of oil in a flat pan until it starts to smoke. Arrange the dumplings (they may need to be cooked in more than 1 batch) in the pan pinched side down, and add enough water to half cover them. Cover the pan and sauté the dumplings for about 5 minutes, or until the bottoms are lightly browned but there is still water in the pan. Turn the dumplings upside down and continue sautéing them until all the water evaporates. Trickle the remaining 3 tbsp of sesame oil into the pan around the dumplings. Turn them over and continue to sauté for 1 or 2 minutes, or until crisp. Remove and set aside. Heat another 1 tbsp of oil and repeat until all the dumplings are cooked.

171. Juicy Steamed Dumplings, Kaifeng Style

4 1/2 (500 g) cups flour, sifted
1 lb (500 g) lean boneless pork, minced
4 tsp soy sauce
1/2 tsp rice wine
1/2 tsp fresh ginger, chopped

2 tsp salt, or to taste
1/2 tsp sugar
4 oz (125 ml) sesame oil
1/2 tsp MSG

1. Mix the pork with the soy sauce, rice wine, ginger, MSG, salt, and sugar. Stir in one direction until it becomes a paste. Stir in the sesame oil and mix well.
2. Add 9 oz (250 ml) of cold water gradually to the flour and mix into a dough. Let rest. Turn out onto a flour board and knead until firm and elastic.
3. Knead the dough again and cut into 1/2 oz (15 g) balls. Flatten each ball lightly with your hand, then roll out each piece into a 3 inch (7 to 8 cm) circle, rotating the dough counter-clockwise while rolling so the centre is slightly thicker than the edges (see Illustration I). Place about 1 to 1 1/2 tbsp (20 g) of filling on each circle and pinch the edges together into 18 pleats (see Illustration II). Place the dumpling in a steamer and steam for 5 minutes over high heat.
Note: These dumplings are delicate in appearance and taste. The wrappers are thin and the filling deliciously juicy.

172. Steamed Pork Dumplings, Tianjin Style

4 1/2 cups (500 g) flour, sifted
4 1/2 tsp baking powder
7 oz (200 g) lean boneless pork, minced
4 tbsp soy sauce

1/2 tsp fresh ginger, chopped
2 tbsp scallions, chopped
7 tsp sesame oil
5 fl oz (140 ml) water for the filling

1. Mix the flour and baking powder with 9 fl oz (250 ml) of water and prepare the dough described in Recipe 170, "Sautéed Dumplings."
2. Mix the pork with the soy sauce and ginger. Gradually add 5 oz (140 ml) of water, 1 1/2 oz at a time, stirring after each addition until the pork becomes a thick paste. Mix in the scallions and sesame oil.
3. Knead the dough and roll into a long roll. Divide it into 30 portions and roll each into a flat circle about 3 inches (7 to 8 cm) in diameter. Divide fillings into 30 portions. Fill with about 1 portion of the pork mixture and seal as in Recipe 171, "Juicy Steamed Dumplings, Kaifeng Style."
4. Place the dumplings in a steamer and steam for 7 minutes. Remove and serve.

173. Pomegranate-Shaped Dumplings (*Shao Mai*), Beijing Style.

4 1/2 cups (500 g) flour, sifted
2 egg whites
1 lb (500 g) lean boneless pork, beef or other meat, diced
5 oz (150 g) cooked meat, diced
3 1/2 tbsp vegetable oil or lard
3 1/2 oz (100 g) canned bamboo shoots, diced
1 tsp shrimp eggs

1 tbsp fresh ginger, chopped
1 tbsp rice wine
2 tsp salt, or to taste
3 1/2 tbsp soy sauce
3 1/2 oz (100 ml) sesame oil
7 oz (200 ml) stock
1 tsp MSG

1. Mix flour with egg whites and water to make a firm dough, following the directions for Recipe 170, "Sauteed Dumplings, Henan Style." Divide the dough into 50 portions and roll each into a circle 5 inches (13 cm) in diameter. Stack 10 fine pieces, one on top of the other. Flour lightly between each of the ten pieces. Press the end of the rolling pin into the dough circularly to make 1 inch (25 mm) long marks (see Illustration I), and separate them to avoid sticking.

2. Heat the oil or lard in a wok until the oil surface ripples. Add the cooked meat and bamboo shoots and stir-fry briefly. Add the shrimp eggs, ginger, 1 tsp of the rice wine, 1 tsp of the salt, and 1/2 tsp of the MSG. Continue to stir-fry 1 minute. Remove and cool. Mix the uncooked meat with the remaining 1/2 tsp of MSG, 1 tsp of the rice wine, 1 tsp of the salt, soy sauce, sesame oil and a little water. Add the bamboo shoots and cooked meat. Mix well. Divide the filling into 50 portions.

3. Take a pastry circle and place 1 portion of the filling in the center. Pull up the edges of the pastry around the filling to make a cylinder, leaving the top open so the filling is visible and the dumpling resembles a pomegranate (see Illustration II). Repeat until all the dumplings are made.

4. Place the dumplings in a steamer and steam for 5 minutes over high heat. Sprinkle with the stock and continue to steam until cooked through. Remove and serve.

174. Steamed Crystal-Filled Dumplings, Beijing Style

4 1/2 cups (500 g) flour
4 1/2 tsp baking powder
2 oz (50 g) pork fat, diced
2 oz (50 g) stir-fried flour
7/8 cup (200 g) sugar
1/3 oz (10 g) walnuts, chopped
1 tsp (5 g) red preserved plum, shredded (optional)
1 tsp (5 g) green preserved plum, shredded (optional)

1. Mix the flour, baking powder, and 9 oz (250 ml) of water into a dough. Let rise, then knead and roll the dough until smooth and elastic. Cut in 10 pieces.
2. Mash the pork fat in a bowl. Mix in the stir-fried flour, sugar, walnuts, preserved plums, and enough water to make a filling (see Illustration I). Divide the filling into 10 portions.
3. Roll out the dough balls into 3 inch (7 cm) circles. Place 1 portion of filling in each wrapper and pinch-gather the edges as illustrated. Steam in a steamer for 7 minutes, or until cooked. Remove and serve.

175. Eight-Treasure Rice (*Babaofan*), Beijing Style

5 oz (150 g) glutinous rice
7/8 cup (200 g) sugar
5 dates, pitted
2 whole green preserved plums
4 preserved white gourd strips
4 dried longan, (shelled and pitted)
25 raisins

10 shelled walnuts
1/2 tsp watermelon seed kernels
10 cooked lotus seeds
1/2 oz (15 g) haw jelly, diced
2 tbsp cornstarch (cornflour), dissolved in 2 tbsp water

1. Wash the rice and place in a heat-proof bowl with 7 oz (200 ml) of water. Place the bowl in a steamer and steam for 25 minutes , or until just cooked. Add half the sugar about 3 1/2 oz (100 g) and mix well. Set aside.
2. Cut the dates, plums, white gourd strips, and dried longan into 1/2 inch (1 cm) cubes. Wash the raisins, shelled walnuts, watermelon seed kernels, and lotus seeds. Set aside.
3. Arrange the fruits and nuts around the sides of a large, greased bowl. Add the cooked rice, which should be level with the bowl's rim. Place in a steamer and steam until the rice is cooked. Cover the bowl with a dish, invert and remove.
4. Mix 1 cup (250 ml) of water and the remaining sugar in a saucepan and bring to a boil. Stir until the sugar dissolves. Add the cornstarch-water mixture and cook, stirring, until it thickens into a thin paste. Pour over the rice, sprinkle with the diced haw jelly, and serve.

176. Sautéed Dumplings (*Guotie* or "Pot-Stickers"), Beijing-Hebei Style

4 1/2 cups (500 g) flour
9 oz (250 g) lean boneless pork, minced
1 tbsp soy sauce
5 tsp rice wine
1 tsp fresh ginger, chopped
1 tsp salt, or to taste
3 1/2 oz (100 g) hotbed leeks
3 1/2 oz (100 ml) sesame oil
1 tsp flour mixed with 2 tbsp water
1 tsp MSG

1. Mix the pork with the soy sauce, rice wine, ginger, MSG and salt. Stir in one direction, adding 5 oz (150 ml) of water, a little at a time until the pork becomes sticky. Add the leeks and sesame oil and blend well, and divide into 60 portions. Set aside.

2. Stir 7 oz (200 ml) of water into the flour. Knead until the dough is smooth and elastic. Let rest for 30 minutes. Roll into a long cylinder and cut into 60 portions. Flatten each piece and roll into a circle about 3 inches (8 cm) in diameter. Place 1 portion of the filling on each circle and fold over. Pinch tightly to seal the edges and form a squat bonnet-shaped pouch (see Illustration I). Repeat until all the dough and filling are used.

3. Arrange the pouches in a large pan (see Illustration II). Heat to moderately hot, then add water to cover the pouches one-third of the way up. Cover the pan and cook over high heat until the water is almost absorbed. Trickle the flour-water mixture around the pouches. Cover the pan and sauté over low heat until the flour forms a crisp film that link the dumplings together. Sprinkle the dumplings with a little sesame oil, cover again, and sauté until the pouches are browned on the bottom. Remove with a spatula and serve. Sauté and serve the dumplings in batches.

177. Boiled Dumplings (*Jiaozi*), Beijing Style

4 1/2 cups (500 g) flour, sifted
10 1/2 oz (300 g) lean boneless pork or mutton, minced
1 tbsp salt, or to taste

6 1/2 tbsp (100 g) scallions, chopped
2 tsp ginger, chopped
1/8 tsp five-spice powder
1/2 tsp MSG

1. Mix the flour with 3 1/2 oz (100 ml) of water to make a dough. Knead until smooth and let stand for 30 minutes.
2. To prepare the filling, mix the pork or mutton with 7 oz (200 ml) of water and the salt. Stir in one direction until it becomes a paste. Add the scallions and blend well. Divide filling into 100 portions.
3. Divide the dough into 4 portions and roll into long rolls. Cut each into 25 pieces. Flatten each piece and roll into 2 inches (5 cm) circles (see Illustration I). Place 1 portion of filling in the center of each wrapper and fold the dough over it, making a bonnet-shaped pouch (see Illustration II). Pinch the edges together to seal the dumpling. Repeat until all the dough and filling are used.
4. Bring 8 cups (2 litres) of water to a boil over high heat. Add half the dumplings. Stir them around gently with a ladel (see Illustration IV), and let the water return to a boil. Add enough cold water to stop the boiling, then bring back to a boil. When the water boils again, add more cold water and bring to a boil a third time. The dumplings will be done when they float to the surface. Remove, drain well, and serve.

178. Pancake with Egg Filling, Kaifeng Style

1 1/2 cups (200 g) flour, sifted
4 eggs
2 tsp scallions, chopped
1 tsp salt, or to taste
7 fl oz (200 ml) vegetable oil

1. Mix the flour with 7 oz (200 ml) of water. Knead until the dough is soft, smooth and elastic.
2. Roll out the dough into a large flat circle. Rub oil all over the surface of the dough, sprinkle with scallions and salt (see Illustration I). Roll the piece away from you. Lift one end, press down to make into a ball. Roll out the ball into a flat circular dough.
3. Place the dough on a heavy frying pan, bake the cake until almost cooked. Lift the cake with one hand and make an opening at the rim. Using the rolling pin to make a hollow inside the cake. Beat eggs and pour into the hollow of the cake. Pinch and seal the opening. Add a little oil to the pan, continue to bake until the eggs inside the cake swell (see Illustration II). Remove and serve.

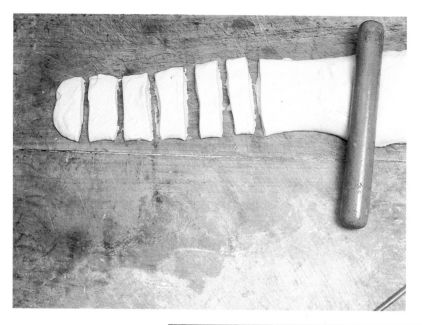

179. Deep-Fried Dough Sticks, Beijing Style

3 1/2 cups (500 g) flour, sifted
4 cups (1,000 ml) vegetable oil for deep-frying
1 tbsp salt, or to taste

1/4 oz (7 g) baking soda
1/2 oz (15 g) alum

1. Dissolve the salt, baking soda and alum in 11 oz (325 ml) of water. Mix the water and flour into a dough. Let stand for 15 minutes, then dampen your hands and knead until the dough is smooth and elastic.
2. Place the dough on an oiled surface and roll into a long strip. Cut into 30 short strips of about 1 oz in weight (see Illustration I). Press two strips together and roll them lengthwise (see Illustration II). Pull the batter sticks until they are 10 inches (24 cm) long.
3. Heat the oil to 400°F (205°C), or until a piece of day-old bread browns in about 30 seconds. Add the dough sticks, a few at a time, and deep-fry, stirring constantly, until brown. Drain well and serve warm with milk or bean milk.

180. Mutton Tarts, Kaifeng Style

4 1/2 cups (500 g) flour, sifted
1 cup (250 ml) vegetable oil
1 1/2 lb (750 g) lean mutton, minced
2 tsp salt, or to taste
4 tsp soy sauce
7 oz (200 ml) mutton stock
9 oz (250 g) cellophane noodles, boiled and

chopped in 1/4 inch (1 cm) sections
3 1/2 tbsp (50 g) scallions, chopped
2 tsp fresh ginger, chopped
1 tbsp (15 ml) sesame oil
1 tsp five-spice powder
1 tsp MSG

1. Mix the mutton with 1 tsp of the salt, soy sauce and stock. Stir in one direction until it becomes a paste, then add the cellophane noodles, scallions, ginger, MSG, sesame oil, and five-spice powder and blend well. Divide the filling into 10 portions. Set aside.

2. Dissolve 1 tsp salt in 10 1/2 oz (300 ml) of water. Stir the water into the flour to make a dough. Knead well. Let stand for a while. Roll the dough into a long roll and cut into 10 round pieces. Roll out each round into a thin circle (see Illustration I). Add 1 portion of the filling to the center of the piece and seal it (see Illustration II). Repeat until all the dough and filling are used.

3. Heat the oil in a pan to about 230°F (110°C), or until small bubbles appear around a piece of ginger or scallion green dropped into the oil. Add the tarts and fry over low heat for 5 minutes, or until the bottoms are brown (see Illustration III). Turn the tarts over and continue to fry for 5 more minutes. Repeat until all the tarts are fried , drain well, and serve.

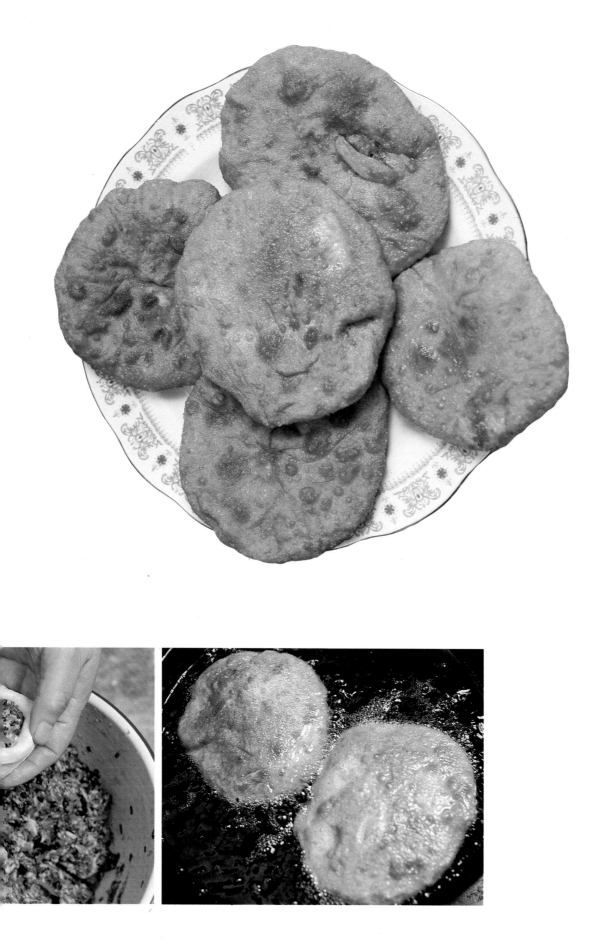

181. Sweetened Dough Twists, Beijing-Tianjin Style

4 1/2 cups (500 g) flour, sifted
5 tbsp brown sugar
2 eggs
10 1/2 oz (300 ml) vegetable oil

1. Mix the flour with 9 oz (250 ml) of water to make a dough.
2. Dissolve the sugar in a little water. Beat the eggs and mix with the sugar. Stir into the dough. Knead the batter until smooth and elastic. Turn onto greased surface and roll into a long roll and cut into 10 round pieces. Roll each piece into a small strip. Fold each strip double and twist into an yarn-like stick.
3. Heat the oil in a wok to about 230°F (110°C). Deep-fry the dough twists slowly until dark brown and crisp. Remove, drain well, and serve.

Sample Menus for a Family Dinner Party

For Chinese families, a meal on a holiday or festive occasion is usually comprised of several special dishes, especially when there are guests. The holiday meal provides an opportunity to display elaborate cooking skills, and to present samplings of a variety of local dishes. The host must consider the personal likes of his guests; some may be especially fond of sweet and sour flavour, others hot and salty; some may prefer chicken and fish dishes while others eat only vegetables. Seasonal factors also influence choice of ingredients. The following are a few sample menus:

Five-dish menus for three or four people:

(1) Twice-Cooked Pork, Sichuan Style (#1)
Piquant Chicken, Sichuan Style (# 60)
Scrambled Eggs with Tomatoes, Beijing Style (#70)
Braised Creamed Cabbage, Tianjin Style (#110)
Muxi Soup, Northeast China Style (#162)

(2) Steamed Spareribs, Beijing Style (#26)
Curried Beef, Guangdong Style (#38)
Dry-Fried Yellow Croaker, Northeast China Style (#80)
Creamy Tomatoes, Hangzhou Style (#108)
Egg-Bubble Soup, Beijing-Hebei Style (#157)

(3) Muxi Pork, Beijing-Northeast China Style (#2)
Braised Beef, Shanxi Style (#39)
Stir-Fried Hot Diced Pork, Beijing Style (#4)
Stir-Fried Spinach, Shanghai Style (#109)
Chinese Cabbage Soup with Dried Shrimps, Shandong Style (#163)

(4) Scrambled Eggs with Pork Slivers, Suzhou Style (#23)
Peppery-Hot Mutton, Northeast China Style (#52)
Fish with Hot Sauce, Beijing Style (#88)
Chinese Yams in Spun Syrup, Shandong Style (#144)
White Fungus Soup, Shandong Style (#159)

Seven-dish menus for five or six people:

(5) Stir-Fried Pork Slices with Scallions, Shandong Style (#15)
Pearly Pork Balls, Beijing-Hebei Style (#12)

Sesame Beef Filet, Northeast China Style (#41)
Egg Dumplings, Chengdu-Sichuan Style (#71)
Oil-Braised Prawns, Beijing Style (#94)
Deep-Fried Yellow Croaker with Sweet-and-Sour Sauce, Shanghai Style (#78)
Peaches in Crystal Syrup, Kaifeng Style (#139)

(6) Steamed Pork Balls, Hangzhou Style (#11)
Deep-Fried Stuffed Green Peppers, Northeast China Style (#32)
Egg Pancakes, Beijing Style (#75)
Tender-Fried Fish Slices, Hangzhou Style (#87)
Deep-Fried Fresh Shrimps, Tianjin Style (#96)
Spicy Bean Curd, Sichuan Style (#128)
Walnut Porridge, Jiangsu Style (#158)

(7) Stir-Fried Diced Pork with Peanuts, Guangdong Style (#16)
Deep-Fried Stuffed Lotus Roots, Shanghai Style (#33)
Braised Beef and Potatoes, Northeast China Style (#44)
Quick-Fried Hot Diced Chicken, Sichuan Style (#68)
Braised Prawns, Shanghai Style (#92)
Sweet-and-Sour Shredded Lotus Roots, Hangzhou Style (#121)
Chicken Velvet Soup, Sichuan Style (#156)

(8) Stir-Fried Pork Cubes with Green Peppers, Beijing Style (#3)
Tender Stewed Beef, Hangzhou Style (#36)
Stewed Chicken Drumsticks, Beijing-Hebei Style (#61)
Stir-Fried Fish Cubes, Shandong Style (#85)
Three Fruits in Syrup, Shandong Style (#145)
Sweet Marinated Lotus Roots, Shandong Style (#150)
Hot-and-Sour Beef Soup, Jiangsu Style (#164)

Index of Recipes

Poultry and Egg Dishes

Fish and Seafood Dishes

Vegetable and Bean Curd Dishes

Sweet Dishes

图书在版编目(CIP)数据

中国家常菜：英文/白自然编；王金怀，雪原撰文. - 北京：外文出版社，1995(2007重印)

ISBN 978-7-119-00407-5

I. 中… II. ①白… ②王… ③雪… III. 菜谱 - 烹饪 - 方法 - 中国 - 英文 IV. TS972.1

中国版本图II书馆CIP数据核字（95）第07516号

中国家常菜

白自然 编

＊

王金怀 雪原 撰文

© 外文出版社出版

（中国北京百万庄路24号）

邮政编码 100037

外文印刷厂印刷

中国国际图书贸易总公司发行

（中国北京车公庄西路35号）

北京邮政信箱第399号 邮政编 100044

1990年（16开）第一版

2008年第一版第九次印刷

（英）

ISBN 978-7-119-00407-5

15000

85-E-299S